Doing the Supernatural Works of Jesus

Proven steps of:
Deliverance, Healing of Emotional Wounds,
Physical Healing, Baptism of the Holy Spirit,
How to stay free and healed

Everett Cox

Copyright © 2010 by Everett Cox

Doing the Supernatural Works of Jesus
Proven steps of: Deliverance, Healing of Emotional Wounds, Physical Healing, Baptism of the Holy Spirit, How to stay free and healed
by Everett Cox

Printed in the United States of America

ISBN 9781612151359

All rights reserved solely by the author. The author guarantees all contents are original and do not infringe upon the legal rights of any other person or work. No part of this book may be reproduced in any form without the permission of the author. The views expressed in this book are not necessarily those of the publisher.

Unless otherwise indicated, Bible quotations are taken from The King James Translation. Copyright ©1981 by Tyndale House Publishers; and The New International Version. Copyright ©1985 by Zondervan Bible Publishers.

www.xulonpress.com

CONTENTS

    PREFACE ix
    DEDICATION xi
    ACKNOWLEDGEMENT ....

1. MORE OF THE GOOD NEWS 13
   Testimony of Everett Cox, a Methodist affected by tragedy. How he pressed in to God for answers, finding comfort in the Comforter. He experienced the same Spirit and the same Jesus that John Wesley was introduced to.

2. MY INTRODUCTION TO DELIVERANCE AND
   HOW I LEARNED TO RECOGNIZE POSSIBLE
   EVIL SPIRITS 17
   Everett Cox learned how to recognize the possibility of evil spirits.

   A COMMON PROBLEM LIST THAT MAY BE NAMES OF SPIRITS
   Most everyone is affected by problems on this list.

3. WHY CHRISTIANS HAVE THE POWER TO WIN 22
   A discussion of the authority of the believer released into our lives by our Lord Jesus Christ.

4. WHY EVIL SPIRITS CAN TORMENT
   CHRISTIANS (THE DOORS) 25
   There are no spiritual vacuums. When we open the door to the devil, he marches right on into our lives to torment us.

   DOORS THAT EVIL SPIRITS OFTEN USE 26
   15 DOORS WE OPEN TO DEMONS 27
   MORE DOORS HAVE BEEN OPENED
   THROUGH THE OCCULT 35

5. THE PRE-MINISTRY PRAYER
   (DOOR CLOSING PRAYER) 36
   This prayer has been a primary key to closing every door the enemy has in our lives so that we can be set free from torment and be healed by Jesus.

6. BREAKING UNGODLY SOUL TIES 41
   Effective ministry can be hindered by ungodly soul ties. This is a four-step process to break those ungodly soul ties so that you can clearly keep the godly ties.

7. DOING INNER HEALING OF PAST WOUNDS 45
   Part of our torment may come from bad memories of terrible experiences or traumas that we have had in life. Jesus reveals Himself to us so that He can speak truth to us to offset any lies we may have bought into.

8. HOW TO MINISTER TO YOURSELF AND OTHERS 49

   ENGAGING AND CASTING OUT EVIL SPIRITS 49
   PRAYING FOR SOMEONE AT A DISTANCE 51

9. HEAD DEMON TECHNIQUE 53
   I learned a technique to reduce the amount of time in ministry and often am able to discover significant keys to their freedom and healing.

10. USE GOD'S ANGELS 59
    We have learned through the years how to effectively use God's angels as ministering spirits sent to serve us.

11. PHYSICAL HEALING 63

    KEYS TO PHYSICAL HEALING 63
    HEALING OF BACKS AND NECKS 64
    ADDITIONAL INSIGHTS INTO PHYSICAL HEALING 66

12. MINISTERING TO CHILDREN 68
    Children are very special to Jesus. This is a guide in how to minister effectively.

13. STEPS TO STAY FREE AND FULL OF LIFE 72

    HOW TO STAY FREE AND HEALED (PART I) 72

DECLARE THESE "I AM" STATEMENTS TO CLEARLY
UNDERSTAND WHO YOU ARE IN CHRIST, TO BUILD
CONFIDENCE IN YOUR FAITH..73
HOW TO STAY FREE AND HEALED (PART II)........................75
DELIVERANCE AND HEALING IN HOLY COMMUNION...........79

14. THE POWER OF GOD 81

WHY THE BAPTISM OF THE HOLY SPIRIT?............................81
Scriptural foundation for the Baptism of the Holy Spirit
and scriptural benefits of this power given to us in the New
Testament.
ADMINISTERING THE BAPTISM OF
THE HOLY SPIRIT WITH SPEAKING IN OTHER TONGUES 83

15. ALL CHRISTIANS ARE CALLED TO
CAST OUT DEMONS 86

NOW IT'S YOUR TURN TO MINISTER WITH
DELIVERANCE HANDOUT 88
    OUR AUTHORITY..88
    DOOR OPENERS 88
    KEYS FOR STAYING FREE 89
    BREAKING UNGODLY SOUL TIES 89
CHECKLIST FOR ONE-ON-ONE MINISTRY............................91
CHECKLIST FOR GROUP INTRODUCTION 92
CHECKLIST FOR GROUP OR MASS DELIVERANCE.............94
MINISTRY REPORT...96

16. STRANGE THINGS I HAVE SEEN DEMONS
SAY AND DO...98
Through the years, I have had many amazing things occur that the
normal person, the person on the street, the normal church member
would never understand.

17. ADDITIONAL THOUGHTS AND OBSERVATIONS 104

ONLY ONE WAY..104
    Jesus is the Way, the Truth and the Life.
HIS DAD CAST IT OUT..105
    Parents have authority to minister to their children.

THE DECEIVER IS AT WORK..106
    Understanding how the deceiver works.
WE CAN SPEAK DIRECTLY TO IT!...108
    We speak to the mountain; we speak to the spirit oppressing us.
    We don't ask Jesus to do it for us.
MOST CHRISTIANS ARE BOTHERED BY DEMONS....................108
    Satan's goal is to contain and contaminate Christian testimony to
    the love of God.
WHO DO YOU KNOW WHO NEEDS A JESUS OVERHAUL?.....109
    You know people in your church, in your family, in your
    neighborhood and at work who are tormented. Jesus can help
    them, too.

18. PROOF OF THE PUDDING – TESTIMONIES..................................111
    Read about individuals who have received ministry and report back
    months or years later that they received effective deliverance from
    panic attacks, fear, fear of flying, fear/insomnia, fear/wrath, seizures,
    healed of Crohn's Disease, heart attack spirit, back pain/neck, thyroid/
    deafness, generational witchcraft, migraine headaches, seeing demons
    in their room, torment as an 11-year-old, grand mal seizures, an old
    and tired spirit, a generational death curse, healed of a frozen neck,
    haunted house, smoking and anger, marriage under attack, a thirteen-
    generation witchcraft spirit, healed of lupus, lesbian set free, homo-
    sexual set free, witchcraft, drug addiction, alcohol addiction, voices of
    suicide, back healed, and anorexia.

19. EXORCISING HOMES, BUILDINGS, OR LAND 126
    Testimonies and a checklist for exorcising a home, buildings or land.

20. MULTIPLE PERSONALITIES 129

    TRUE MULTIPLE PERSONALITIES ARE NOT DEMONS............129
    PROTECTOR, ALTERNATE PERSONALITY, MPD,
    DID, SRA CHECKLIST 132

PREFACE

The Lord has impressed upon me to equip an army with teaching the basics of the door-closing, followed with the three ministry steps of breaking of ungodly soul ties, inner healing, and working the problem list. I have seen thousands set free through this simple method of ministry. I have found it is an easy ministry method to teach and can be networked into the Christian churches.

This book (manual) is for all born again Christians. All Christians can follow these proven steps and see amazing results, often in one session. A special spiritual gift is not needed. The Word of God performs itself as Christians speak it. These seasoned and field tested steps are used by me and our teams at our Monday evening one on one sessions. These steps will work with most people as you learn how to minister to someone else or yourself. Yes, many Christians can do self ministry. You can activate your faith to deliver yourself from evil spirits (including spirits of infirmity). You can minister inner healing of past emotional wounds, physical healing and receive the Baptism of the Holy Spirit or minister to someone else as they receive.

I wish to acknowledge Pastor John Benefiel, who today is the senior pastor of The Church on the Rock in Oklahoma City. He and two other pastors administered the Baptism of the Holy Spirit to me after I had lost a child in 1978 and gave me my initial full gospel spiritual base. An old childhood friend of mine, Dr. Lynn Myers had sent them over to pray for me. I am so thankful they were there for me ... what if they had not been there? That day I received the comforter and got the power for spiritual service!

I also want to acknowledge the late Frank Hammond who wrote the <u>Pigs in the Parlor</u> and numerous other deliverance books. Brother Frank was a guest on my radio show many times. I even sponsored him into Oklahoma City for large deliverance meetings when our ministry was getting started. As a personal friend, he was available to me by telephone as questions came up through the years.

I developed a personal friendship with Dr. Charles Kraft. He has authored many books on inner healing and deliverance. Dr. Kraft was a professor with Fuller Theological Seminary in Pasadena, California for many years and greatly strengthened my spiritual base. I also sponsored him for teaching and ministry sessions in Oklahoma City. He too was a guest on my radio show numerous times.

A special appreciation to Pastor Richard Hogue and City Church of Oklahoma City for allowing Deliverance Ministries, Inc. to hold Monday evening ministry sessions for over a decade.

Also, I want to thank Richard and Mary Jo Peterson, Linda and Trey Merrick, George and Kay Williams and Kelli Schick for their contributions to the content and editing of this book.

Everett Cox
Sr. Minister and Founder
Deliverance Ministries, Inc.
www.delmin.org

DEDICATION

I feel that each person who is set free and healed through the ministry described herein, and the associated networking of the ministers, is a tribute to my daughter, Lori ... for it is because of her death that I reached out to the fullness of the Gospel and ultimately founded Deliverance Ministries, Inc.

CHAPTER 1

MORE OF THE GOOD NEWS

There are many Christians who have certain problem areas in their lives. They have never received their victory in areas that torment them, including fear, anger or rage, chronic depression, stress, anxiety, addictions, perversions, wounds of the past, and many physical infirmities. Some are sick all the time. The good news is that you can be set free and healed by applying information contained in this book. You can also learn how to minister to others with the same results.

Find out how these scriptures, methods and proven techniques can work for every Christian. Jesus really did mean it when He said in John 14:12, "He that believeth on me, the works that I do shall he do also; and greater than these shall he do; because I go to my Father."

Just doing "the works of Jesus" is amazing. Doing "greater works" seemed inconceivable to me in the beginning. What you are about to read and learn about fall into the category of "greater works." The various testimonies are proof of the pudding. This is normal Christianity, not some special gift given to a few ... NORMAL CHRISTIANITY!

Now, I'm not a graduate of a seminary. I'm not a priest. Instead, I have a BBA degree from the University of Oklahoma in finance. In addition, I have numerous post-graduate courses and a vocational background in mortgage banking. I am a businessman who "does the works of Jesus."

How do I qualify to do the "works of Jesus"? I have only one qualification ... I'm a BELIEVER! A believer in Jesus ... a born again Christian. And, guess what? If you are a born again believer, YOU QUALIFY ALSO! Jesus gave us commands in Mark 16 that signs (**supernatural signs**) shall follow those who **believe**, to cast out demons, to speak with new tongues, to lay hands on the sick and they shall recover. The New Testament clearly says that after Jesus arose to sit on the right hand of God, they (**the believers**) went forth preaching everywhere. The Lord worked with them confirming the Word with signs (**supernatural signs**) following. I had no idea that the supernatural was going to be such a major part of my future. I was not aware that I would experience doing these works of Jesus, in His Name, personally.

I was born again when I was 13, however, I never really grew as a Christian. Even though I always had a childlike belief that the Bible was the word of God, I was a nominal, denominational Christian attending church most Sundays. I never spent a lot of time reading the Word. I knew the Lord's Prayer. My parents taught me the Lord's Prayer as a child. I did recite it before going to sleep often. (That probably kept me out of trouble more than I know).

I was more caught up in the activities of the world through those years. I cowboyed some, had a nice sorrel quarter horse with a trailer, did some rodeo calf roping and worked on some ranches through the years. I got interested in electronics and received my amateur radio license. I bicycled through Europe one summer while I was in college. I spent another summer in Southeast Asia with a group from Oklahoma University. After graduating from Oklahoma University, I was accepted at the Naval Officers Candidate School in Newport, Rhode Island. As a naval officer I attended numerous Navy schools. I married and spent 2-1/2 years on Guam with an airborne early warning squadron. I did a lot of skin diving when I was stationed on Guam. I finally returned to Oklahoma in 1960 and joined my father in mortgage banking.

I continued pursuing the worldly activities and what adventure it offered through the following 18 years. We had three wonderful daughters. I was CEO and major stockholder of a large mortgage banking company. I owned and piloted four airplanes through the years, including an aerobatic aircraft and a turbo-charged pressurized Cessna 421. I was skin diving the Bahamas, the Marshall Islands, the Eastern Carolines (now Micronesia), even a Spanish galleon that sank in 1741 off Yucatan, and recovered artifacts. I enjoyed snow skiing during the years we owned a condo in Breckenridge, Colorado. I hunted and fished all over North America including Alaska … always seeking fulfillment and adventure. Life was on a roll … so I thought.

Tragedy struck on March 15th, 1978. That was when I lost my 18-year-old daughter. My oldest daughter, Lori, had been tormented with seizures since she was about 10 years old. Using medication, she didn't have them often. She may have had one seizure a year. Of course, that didn't slow her down at all. She did everything she wanted to do. Lori was captain of the drill team in high school. She was majoring in ballet at the University of Oklahoma. And of course, we kept thinking that the medications would make it so that she would not have any re-occurrence at all.

In March of 1978, Lori went with a group of friends from the university to Crested Butte, Colorado. After a hard skiing day, Lori chose to relax in a Jacuzzi. Her girl friend had stepped into the shower. I'll never forget that phone call ... when someone told me that Lori had a seizure and drowned in the Jacuzzi. My world came crashing down on me.

The agony of losing a child is one of the worst pains that there is ... I felt devastating grief month after month after month, with no relief in sight. All I felt was pain and I was paralyzed with that pain. A close friend of mine, whom I have known since the second grade, Dr. Lynn Myers, a pathologist, felt that he knew something that would offer me comfort. He sent several pastors from his Full Gospel church over to my house on a Saturday afternoon. The first thing they said was, "What you need is the Baptism of the Holy Spirit." I remember saying, "What's that?"

These pastors opened up the Bible and started showing me various scriptures. As I looked at these passages of scripture, I could see that there may be some validity to their claim that Jesus baptizes with the Holy Spirit. It did seem that the scriptures described another baptism in addition to the water baptism that I had experienced many years ago. These pastors showed me that when the Holy Spirit comes in His fullness, He comes as a comforter (John 16:7). I knew I needed something. I seemed to have a big hole of agony inside me that needed filling. Any comfort would be wonderful.

These pastors showed me in Acts 2:4 that when the Holy Spirit came down on the Christians who were waiting in the upper room, "they spoke with other tongues as the Holy Spirit gave them utterance." They showed me in Luke 11:9-13 that I could ask for the Holy Spirit and receive the fullness of the Holy Spirit by faith in the same way I received Jesus as Savior so many years ago. Now, I had heard of speaking in tongues. I had always thought it sounded weird ... but at this point, I didn't care. I needed relief from the pain. They led me through a prayer asking Jesus to baptize me with the Holy Spirit. As these pastors began to speak in tongues over me, the next thing I knew was that I began speaking some words that I didn't understand! A relief and inner peace came upon me. This peace I couldn't understand ... but I sure took it (Philippians 4:7). That was on June 17, 1978, the date that revolutionized my life forever!

Even though I had the GOOD NEWS of my salvation at the age of 13, now, at the age of 44, I received more of the GOOD NEWS. The Comforter had come in His fullness to change my life forever.

It didn't take me long to realize that the Holy Spirit comes with more than comfort. He comes with a whole package! I immediately seemed to have a power to witness about what I had received and to talk about Jesus. (Acts 1:8, "But ye shall receive power, after that the Holy Ghost is come upon you and ye shall be witnesses...") I also had a hunger for the Word that was brand new to me. Yes, it finally hit me that I had received a whole package from the Holy Spirit! I have not been the same since.

I somehow knew, inside of me, that I was to be doing the works of Jesus. Now I needed to learn what works He did. In time, I learned more of this

GOOD NEWS. I found out that I would be leading people to a saving knowledge of Jesus. I began doing and teaching deliverance from evil spirits that oppress godly people. I began ministering physical and emotional healing.

In addition, I am administering the Baptism of the Holy Spirit. I founded Deliverance Ministries, Inc. in 1984 and have been leading that ministry since then. We do the "SUPERNATURAL" works of Jesus. We now train teams to minister the good news of Jesus, that He sets the captives free. I hosted a pre-taped weekday radio interview show about these works of Jesus for 22 years.

The excitement of sharing the GOOD NEWS … to discover that some of our problems are just evil spirits … to begin understanding doors we open to demonic activity, including generational doors … to find the answer in Jesus' name … to achieve victory in Jesus. What an adventure!

I quickly saw that the people we ministered to were born again, spirit-filled Christians. We ministered to people whose spirits were secure in Jesus, possessed by Jesus. But, evil spirits were tormenting them in their physical body and their soul. (The soul is made up of the mind, will and emotions.) 1Thessalonians 5:23 points out how we have these three parts, "And the very God of peace sanctify you wholly; and *I pray God* your whole spirit and soul and body be preserved blameless unto the coming of our Lord Jesus Christ."

Over a quarter of a century has passed … I have been living the greatest adventure of my life. With this said, I am also enjoying supernatural fulfillment, too. And here is your GOOD NEWS, if you will follow these simple steps … the simple steps I am outlining in this book … you, too, will see "SUPERNATURAL" signs following you … **this is for all Christians**.

CHAPTER 2

MY INTRODUCTION TO DELIVERANCE AND HOW I LEARNED TO RECOGNIZE POSSIBLE EVIL SPIRITS

Shortly after I received the baptism of the Holy Spirit in 1978, my friend, Dr. Lynn Myers told me more about his little Full Gospel church. The members were doing the works of Jesus, including casting out evil spirits. I felt that I really needed to see this. Frankly, I really needed to see it to believe it. After all, this is the modern space age. Demons ... today? Give me a break!

Dr. Myers was able to make it possible for me to sit in on ministry at his church. I sat in on several cases of deliverance. **Finally I saw my first demon manifestation.** (A demon acting out or speaking out of a person) I'll never forget this man who was a born again Christian, about 40 years old. The minister asked the man what was bothering him, what were the problems in his life. As this man spoke, I noticed the minister, with a yellow tablet in hand, writing down suspect spirits by their problem names. I thought, "How easy."

It has now been over three decades since that event. The man mentioned some problems, at least a couple dozen problems; so, the minister wrote those down. Anger and rage were discussed ... those went on the suspect list. The pastor quoted some scriptures. Finally, Pastor John began ministry ... commanding each suspect spirit, one at a time, to come out in Jesus' Name. As the minister was addressing a particular suspicious spirit, suddenly the man's face contorted ... his mouth tightened up ... I could see his eyes glaring at me. Then his voice sounded different than his own natural voice with which he had been speaking so matter-of-fact earlier. His voice sounded angry and mean.

I was looking at this ... wondering ... thinking in the back of my mind that all this surely was mental ... but he looked really weird, with his face all contorted. This is what convinced me: The pastor said to the voice coming out of this Christian's mouth, "Now, who is your master? Who do you serve?" The voice answered immediately, "Satan." That is when it soaked in: "My God, this is real! This is the manifestation of a demon!" I knew this born again Christian would never say that voluntarily! Jesus is his Lord. So, who is speaking about serving Satan? Well, it's not too hard to figure out who it is when the voice says that its master is "Satan."

At this point I decided, "If I am in a spiritual war zone, maybe I should learn how to shoot." (I enjoy hunting and fishing every year. I knew how to shoot a gun. I did not know how to shoot spiritually.) So, during the following weeks, I went around to the Christian bookstores and found out that even in 1978, the "Full Gospel Christian bookstores" had whole sections of books on "How to cast out evil spirits in the Name of Jesus." I didn't even know all this was going on! I felt somewhat shocked and short-changed. I was born again when I was 13 and was in mainline denominational churches through the years from age 13 to age 44.

However, I had never even heard about the practicality and validity of this work of Jesus. Nor did I hear about His commands for believers to do the same works Jesus did; i.e., set the captives free, commanding evil spirits to leave an individual's soul (mind, will, or emotions) or physical body (Mark 16:17). We know that when we are born again, our spirit comes alive and Jesus lives in our heart (our spirit). Our soul has to be transformed by the renewing of our mind. (Rom 12:1-2)

As months went by, I kept sitting in on more deliverances and reading books on the subject. I finally joined that little Full Gospel Church. Then the day came when I felt comfortable in leading in the ministry of deliverance and saw amazing results! For six years I ministered to Christians, including children. Finally, I formed the non-profit corporation, Deliverance Ministries, Inc. We have done Monday evening weekly teaching and ministry using teams since 1984.

Who am I to do this? I'm not a seminary graduate ... I'm not a priest ... instead, I'm a businessman with a financial and real estate background. But I did have the <u>primary</u> biblical qualification ... **I'm a Born Again Believer!** Remember, if you are a born again believer, then you too are qualified to set the captives free, heal the sick, and do the works of Jesus in His name. (John 14:12)

My belief is that this book will give you the confidence to step out into His supernatural signs and miracles. You will also quickly see that the best defense is an offense.

Recognizing evil spirits is the easy part of this ministry.

You will tend to know them by what they are trying to do. "You will know them by their fruit." (Matthew 7:17) Of course, in the case of demons, by their bad fruit. So, if someone has a problem with fear, there is likely

to be a spirit of fear. If someone has an anger problem, there is likely to be a spirit of anger, etc. We will tend to know them by what they are trying to do in our lives.

As you will see in the following chapters, the <u>greatest challenge</u> is in trying to figure out what the spirits have as their "open doors". An open door is a "root" or "legal right" that the spirit has to harass, torment or oppress an individual. We must deal with these before engaging evil spirits to cast them out.

Over the years I have seen certain "open doors" to be quite common. These "open doors" are usually present. More often than not, I have seen unforgiveness as a major door. This is why going through the door-closing prayer makes such a big difference. The door-closing prayer makes the difference in having an easy and lasting ministry session.

Remember, it is great news to discover that some of our problems are driven by evil spirits. At last, we have a real biblical answer and can do something about it.

The following is a list that we hand out to those who come to us for ministry. This list serves as a worksheet for individual ministry. We will have natural levels of many of the problems listed; however, we suggest you circle what tends to be overboard, out of balance, or tormenting. These are possibly influenced by demons.

CIRCLE THE FOLLOWING THAT ARE A PROBLEM OR IF YOU HAVE HAD INVOLVEMENTS:

ANTICHRIST
Rebellion, Stubbornness
False Prophet Spirit
ANGER
Rage, Wrath
Irrational Anger, Self Anger
Temper
Violence
BITTERNESS *
Hate
Self-Hate
Unforgiveness, of self
Hurt
Resentment
Revenge
Retaliation
Jealousy, Envy*
Murder
BONDAGE
Hyperactivity, Overbearing, Talkative,
Impatience
Stealing (Kleptomania)
Physical pain, victim
Blocked Emotion, Affection
Blocked Completion, Frigidity
Physical Cold or Hot.
Workaholic, Perfectionism
Trauma,* Birth Trauma
Racism
Tension Headache, Migraine
Insomnia
Compulsions, Competition
Unclean, Messiness, Hording
Bulimia, Anorexia
Arson, Fascination with fire
Finger Nail biting
Hair twisting/pulling
CONDEMNATION *
Guilt
Unworthiness
Accusations*
Inferiority*
Insecurity*
Shame
Shyness, Timidity
Embarrassment
Intimidation, Over sensitive

CONFUSION *
Forgetfulness
Mind Control
Mind Blocking
Mind Hindering
Soul Fragmenting
Indifference, Double Mindedness
Procrastination
Illiteracy
CONTROL
Ruler
Manipulation
Chauvinism
Possessiveness
Domineering
CRAVINGS &ADDICTIONS*
Alcohol
Nicotine
Drugs
Medications
Gluttony, Food, Sweets
Over eating, Fear of starvation
Caffeine
Affection
Sex, Pornography
Gambling
Craving of Things
Torment by withdraw   Idolatry of
above
DEATH *
Death Wish
Suicide
Murder, Abortion
By Infirmity*
By Accident*, Driving too fast
DECEPTION* (Accepting lies)
Self-deception
Delusion, blinding
Deceit, Denial
Lies to the mind*
DESTROYER *
Withdrawal,
Separation
Of relationships, Of Marriages
Compromise, Division, Divorce
Self-destruction, Self mutilation
Failure, tragedy, Sabotage

DEAF & DUMB
Seizures, Convulsions
Deafness-physical/spiritual
DOUBT/DISBELIEF
Skepticism, Unbelief
FATIGUE
Tiredness
Laziness
Insomnia
Despondency
Weakness
Lethargy
Sleepiness
Slumbering
Old and tired
FALSE COMPASSION & RESPONSIBILITY
Co-dependency
Need to rescue/false burden
FALSE PROPHESY
False voices
FEAR*
of Abandonment
of Death
of Driving
of Future
of Poverty
of Spiders, of Insects, Snakes
of Man, of Woman, of People
of Animals
of Disapproval, Not good enough
of Confrontation
of Germs, of Sickness
of Satan
of Going Outside
of Rejection, of public speaking
of Authority, of Doctors
of Success
of Dark
of Height
of Love
of Loneliness
of Commitment
of being hurt, of Failure
of Trusting
All phobias, Panic attacks
Fear of:_____

Doing the Supernatural Works of Jesus

HEAVINESS / STRESS *
Depression
Grief, Sorrow
Sadness
Hopelessness
Worry
Anxiety, Nervousness
Stress, Pressure, Tension
Crying
Heartache
Defeatism, **Unloving***
Self-Pity, Pouting
Emotional Pain
Despair, disappointment
Entrapment
Loneliness
LYING *
To Others, Exaggeration
To Self, **Demons of the lies***
Satanic lie program*
IDOLATRY (False God)
Self
People, Pets
Things, Money
Hobbies, Games, Sports
Business/work/computer
Facebook, Twitter
Cell phone, texting
Lifestyle, Entertainment, TV
Problems, Sickness
Past
American Indian Ways
Food
Sex
Alcohol, Drugs
Others:_____
INFIRMITY
(May include any disease or sickness- be specific-address them by their medical names)
Unrepented sin and unforgiveness are typical doors -
Inner-healing usually needed
JEZEBEL
Seductive Behavior
Witchcraft
Manipulation, Control
LEVIATHAN
(Blocks mind, Bible study, Prideful)
MENTAL ILLNESS
Madness
Mania (hyperactivity)
Retardation
Deaf & Dumb
Schizophrenia, Bi-polar
Paranoia
Hallucinations
Manic Depression

MOCKERY
Folly, Funny
STEALING, Cheating
MULTIPLE YOU
Use inner healing for traumas.
(Finally, pray for the real you that was made in God's image to come up in you and stay)
REJECTION *
Fear of Rejection
Self-Rejection
Rejection in the Womb
PERVERSION
Lust
Fantasy, Sadistic
Lesbianism
Homosexuality
Masturbation
Adultery, Abuse of children
Molestation
Incest
Incubus, Sucubus
Harlotry
Rape
Exposure, Beastiality
Pornography
POVERTY
Financial Bondage, Blockage, Destruction, Cash stealing, Lack
PRIDE
Haughtiness
Ego
Intellectualism
Leviathan
Vanity
Self-Righteousness
Importance
Spiritual Pride
Arrogance
PROFANITY
Cursing
Blasphemy
Taking God's Name in vain
REBELLION
Self-Will
Stubbornness
Disobedience
Anti-Submissiveness
RELIGION
Tradition, Doctrines, Ritualism
Legalism, Formalism
Martial Arts, False Religions
Yoga and the spirit Kundalini
Secret Societies, KKK
Free Masonry, Eastern Star
SELF
Selfishness, Self gratification
Self Will, Self righteousness

STRIFE
Conflict
Bickering
Argument
Quarreling
Fighting
Criticism
Judgment
Gossiping
Accusation
Faultfinding
Meanness, Cruelness
TORMENT
Harassment
Nightmares
WITCHCRAFT/OCCULT*
Ouija
Familiar Spirits, Spirit Guide
Palmistry
Divination, Sorcery
Horoscopes/Astrology
Fortunetelling
Worship of the Dead
Charms, Crystals
Tarot cards, Pendulum
Voodoo, Wicca, Santeria
Medicine Man Spirits
Indian Witchcraft, Shamanism
Psychic, Séance
Witchcraft Control
Others:_____
Address those groups marked with an as trek (*) Also the **"Gatekeeper"**
Cancel all satanic assignments and command all demons of the assignments to go.

Ungodly Soul Ties to be broken:
Dad, Mom, Family members

Ex-spouse(s)

Spouse

Sexual Group, Sexual Abuse, Rape

Others that have hurt you a lot, excessive control over you or out of balance relationship:
_____
_____
_____
_____

OTHERS:
_____
_____
_____
_____
_____

CHAPTER 3

WHY CHRISTIANS HAVE THE POWER TO WIN

There is a direct chain of command from Almighty God to Christians today, giving us His power and authority to preach the Kingdom of God, to cast out demons, and to heal the sick.

This chain of command comes through the Holy Spirit from God the Father to God the Son, to the twelve disciples, to the seventy, to <u>ALL who believe</u>.

ALL WHO BELIEVE! THAT'S US!!

Here is how it works, directly from God's Holy Word:

THE AUTHORITY OF JESUS

"In the beginning was the Word" (Jesus)."..and the Word was with God, and the Word was God (John 1:1).

."..and the Word was made Flesh..." (John 1:14).

"I and My Father are one" (John 10:30).

"All power has been given unto Me in heaven and in earth." (Matthew 28:18)

"The Spirit of the Lord is upon Me, because He hath anointed Me to preach the gospel to the poor, He hath sent me to heal the brokenhearted, to preach deliverance to the captives, and the recovering of sight to the blind, to set at liberty them that are bruised. To preach the acceptable year of the Lord" (Luke 4:18-19).

"The thief cometh not, but to steal, and to kill, and to destroy: I am come that they might have life, and that they have it more abundantly" (John 10:10).

"For this purpose the Son of Man was manifested, that He might destroy the works of the devil" (1 John 3:8).

TO THE TWELVE

"Then He (Jesus) called His twelve disciples together, and gave them power and authority over ALL devils, and to cure diseases. And He sent them to preach the kingdom of God and to heal the sick" (Luke 9:1-2).

TO THE SEVENTY

After these things the Lord appointed other seventy also, and sent them two and two before His face into every city and place, whether He Himself would come.

"And the seventy returned again with joy, saying, Lord, even the devils are subject unto us through Thy Name. And He said unto them, 'I beheld Satan as lightning fall from heaven. Behold, I give unto you power to tread on serpents and scorpions and over **ALL** the power of the enemy: and nothing shall by any means hurt you'" (Luke 10:1, 17-19).

TO THOSE WHO BELIEVE

"And these signs shall follow them that believe; in My Name shall they cast out devils; they shall speak with new tongues; they shall take up serpents; and if they drink any deadly thing, it shall not hurt them; they shall lay hands on the sick and they shall recover" (Mark 16:17-18).

"And they went forth, and preached everywhere, the Lord working with them, and confirming the word with signs following" (Mark 16:20).

"And ye are complete in Him, who is the head of all principality and power" (Colossians 2:10).

THAT'S IT! OUR DIRECT LINE OF AUTHORITY FROM OUR HEAVENLY FATHER to cast out devils, to preach His kingdom, to heal the sick. (1st) First to Jesus, the Word who was with God, and is God, (2nd) then to the Twelve, (3rd) then to the Seventy, (4th) and now to ALL WHO BELIEVE. And as believers we have **ALL** power in His Name! **"ALL"** means not 50% or 75% but **100% power and authority in His Name**.

I love Mark 16:20, where the believers went forth with the **Lord, confirming His word with signs following**. I have seen His word confirmed for over three decades now with supernatural signs, since most people experience them in our ministry times. Some of the most common are coughs, burps, yawns and physically feeling the evil spirits depart. We often see a short leg or arm adjust as we speak in the Name of Jesus. Yes, these are supernatural signs!

Without question, "Heaven and earth shall pass away, but My words shall never pass away" (Matthew 24:35). "Jesus Christ, the same yesterday, today, and forever" (Hebrews 13:8).

Many Christians have not realized who they are in Jesus and about this power. Of course, the power is only realized when the Christian applies it... when the word is spoken... when we speak in a specific way. We have

sold ourselves way too short in what can happen when we, as believers, speak in the Name of Jesus!

CHAPTER 4

WHY EVIL SPIRITS CAN TORMENT CHRISTIANS (THE DOORS)

How do we come under the influence of demons? The common entry: **Christians open doors if we do not obey the Word of God.** Many years ago now, there was a brown cat that lived next door, but it used to come over to our patio from time to time. I made the mistake of putting a bowl of milk out through our sliding doors once. Once was all it took. From then on, that cat was hanging around our house and even trying to come through that door into our house. If that door was just slightly cracked, it would shoot in.

The devil is like that. If we open a door, he will come right in. Again, **doors are opened if we don't obey the Word of God. Unforgiveness is the most common open door; i.e., choosing to not proactively forgive others and ourselves. We can also be affected by doors opened by our ancestors; their sins and iniquities ... who has escaped having some type of generational curse? And then there are curses (including generational) spoken by witches and others. Demons ride in on the curses.**

Through the years, we have also seen the results of **satanic assignments** put on Christians who have a strong anointing and many God-given gifts. Most Christians never deal with this problem; they just sit there wondering why they don't get free of certain torments, problems and sicknesses. **The good news:** assignments and curses are easily broken because of the power we have in Christ. (Luke 10:19) The next step we take is to command (rebuke) the demons of the curses and/or assignments to go to the feet of Jesus. We get as specific as we can.

It should be made clear that Christians cannot be "possessed" by demons – certainly not in our born again spirits, but we can be bothered in the flesh and our soul. The term "possessed" does not even exist in the Greek. It is a bad translation. "Diamonizomi" is the Greek word in the Bible that means "under the influence of a demon or demonized." God's Word says we are made with spirit, soul and body. 1 Thessalonians 5:23 says, "And the very God of peace sanctify you wholly; and I pray your whole **spirit, soul**, and **body** be preserved blameless unto the coming of our Lord Jesus Christ." Many people forget that we have these three parts.

So our spirits are secure as born again Christians, but these evil spirits are tormenting us in the body and the soul area (mind, will and emotions). For 30 years, I have observed the majority of Christians receiving ministry actually feel the evil spirits moving around in their body and finally coming out. Certainly, this is a "sign and wonder."

James told Christians to resist (James 4:7), as did Peter (1 Peter 5:8-9). So, let's submit to God and His Word and resist the devil as needed to be freed up, so we can enjoy the abundant life and move forward in our ministries. Just remember that if we want easy and lasting ministry, these entries or doors the demons have used must be closed **first,** so as to **cut any roots** and **cancel any legal rights** the evil spirits might have to return. This is why we use the "door-closing prayer" before ministry. This door-closing prayer is available on the web site at www.delmin.org, by clicking on the link, or in DVD or CD format at the office, or on Monday night in Oklahoma City, OK when we have regularly scheduled ministry time from 5.30 pm to 10.30 pm.

DOORS THAT EVIL SPIRITS OFTEN USE

Christians are an obvious threat to Satan and his demons. Christians with special, anointed gifts to the body of Christ are especially a threat to Satan. As a result, through the interrogation of demons as mentioned in the previous chapter, we have discovered that at least 1/3 of the demons we have cast out are there by **satanic assignment** to block the Christians' life, their gifting, their ministries and certainly the abundant life that they are promised to experience. The good news is that assignments are easy to break since we have **"ALL"** power in Jesus' Name when we use it! (Luke 10:19) We break satanic assignments in the pre-ministry door-closing prayer. The majority of the other evil spirits have entered the soul or the body through various doors that Christians have opened to the devil, including curses, generational curses, or other types of curses spoken by believers, unbelievers and witches.

It is very important to be aware that we are called to be holy, even as Jesus is holy. Ephesians 1 is very clear that we are predestined to be holy and to be conformed to the image of Jesus, Himself. We do this by walking in the Spirit. (Romans 8) However, because we are human, we blow it, we do our own thing instead of doing His thing, and open doors to the enemy of our souls to come under his influence instead of under Jesus' influence. This is how we become oppressed. Demons or evil spirits enter the soul or physical body of believers when Christians open doors to the enemy.

15 DOORS WE OPEN TO DEMONS

This is a list of 15 doors that enable evil spirits to begin influencing the believer. These doors can be closed though declaration and prayer as discussed in Chapter 6 entitled "THE PRE-MINISTRY PRAYER (DOOR-CLOSING PRAYER)"

1) IGNORING THE NEED TO BE BORN AGAIN

Obviously, if you are not born again, you have no power over the enemy. Unless you have put yourself under the authority of the Lord Jesus, the demons are not under your authority in His name. Jesus said in John 3:3:

"Verily, verily I say unto thee, Except a man be born again, he cannot see the kingdom of God." Jesus also said in verse 5: "Except a man be born of water (we were all born out of a sack of water) AND of the Spirit, he cannot enter the Kingdom of God."

So how do we become born again? Romans 10:9-11 tells us:

"That if thou shalt confess with thy mouth the Lord Jesus, and shalt believe in thine heart that God raised Him from the dead, thou shalt be saved. For with the heart man believeth unto righteousness; and with the mouth confession is made unto salvation. For the scripture saith, Whosoever believeth on Him shall not be ashamed." KJV

If you are not sure that you are born again… **sincerely** pray the sinner's prayer out loud during the door closing prayer.

2) UN-REPENTED SIN

Sin is clearly a door for Satan. We are told in the scriptures to "Sin not… give no place to the devil" (Ephesians 4:26-27). When a person is born again, his sin, of course, is totally washed away with that free gift by grace from the cross. It is not of works that we do (religious activity) but by what Jesus did for us… a free gift (Ephesians 2:8)! How awesome that Jesus took our sin for us as the final sacrificial Lamb! We stand totally righteous before the Father at that point. I am the righteousness of God in Christ Jesus.

Then time starts passing, hours, days, weeks, months, maybe years later… there are Christians who have been known to blow it and sin later. Do you know of a Christian who has not sinned later? I always have to raise my hand with this question. I am not proud that I have messed up, but I am excited when I read scriptures. 1 John 1:9 says, "If we confess our sins, He is faithful and just to forgive us and to cleanse us of all unrighteousness." The key to this happening is that we are **sincere** in our repentance. One of the most basic doctrines of the church is found in Hebrews 6… repentance from dead works and faith toward God. The process of repentance, confession of sin and forgiveness is a basic habit of the Christian. And of course, God will know if we are sincere because He is God!

The point is that, yes, Christians sin again (duh!) and there are a large number who have not got around to repentance. So, they have a opened a door to the demonic to enter through this "Un-repented sin door." Repenting will be in the pre-ministry door-closing prayer.

3) UNFORGIVENESS

I think this is the **by far the most common of all the doors**. It impacts people in a powerful way. I might add … the most insidious and illusive. This is the entry that I have goofed up on by carrying resentment and hurts. The flesh is quick to want revenge when we have been wronged, or when we think we have been wronged, OR hurt. Demonic activity is quick to come into our souls, our mind, our will, our emotions, our imaginations or our physical body with any door that is opened. Jesus said, "If you do not forgive you will be turned to the **tormentors**" (Matthew 18:34-35). Who do you think are the tormentors? It would be around **three dozen evil spirits** like what you see on the problem list in Chapter 3.

You might say, "You don't know what the person has done to me." I am sure if you told me what was done to you, I would probably agree he/she does not deserve to be forgiven. However, neither did we deserve forgiveness from God, the Father. So, if you want to be delivered from the tormentors, it is "choice" time for you. Forgiveness is a choice even though the feelings may linger. You can override the feelings and just DO IT! God made you with the ability to have free choice. **You can choose anything! So, choose to forgive.**

Consider a train. There is an engine that pulls the train and a caboose that is normally the last car on the train following the engine wherever the engine chooses to go. Choice is comparable to the engine. Emotions are comparable to the caboose. When you make choices, your emotions will eventually follow because the driving force of our lives is "choice."

Forgiving yourself is just as important as forgiving others. Blaming God for something is another door the enemy will use. We choose to forgive God, forgive ourselves and forgive others. We do not do it based on the fact that they deserve to be forgiven. We choose to forgive so we set ourselves free from the prison of unforgiveness. I have seen demons use these entries many times. It is not worth holding unforgiveness or resentment against anyone, because it hurts us in the end.

ESPECIALLY IMPORTANT: **Spirits of sickness, weakness or infirmity** use the unforgiveness door as a primary entry door in most cases. Would you call cancer or lupus a tormentor? Often, when I have ministered to someone with a major disease, I may be ministering for an hour or two before the deep-rooted bitterness is finally disclosed. Sometimes it is from something they experienced as a child. Once the person deals with the memory foundation of unforgiveness, deliverance and healing can take place.

At the end of the door-closing prayer, I will lead you to ask the Lord to show you who you need to forgive. Jesus is good at putting names and faces into our minds when we ask Him to. Of course, it will be up to you to tell Jesus that you forgive that person. Once you forgive, it is most important to follow up forgiveness with blessing those you have forgiven. As He (Jesus) keeps showing you who you need to forgive, just keep forgiving and blessing until no more names or faces come to your mind or heart. **You do not want one ounce of unforgiveness left inside your heart!**

4) REFUSING TO HONOR YOUR FATHER AND MOTHER SO YOU WILL HAVE LONG LIFE

Choosing an attitude of honor may be difficult to do, due to problems and things that have happened with your parents. In your mind, your parents may not deserve to be honored; however, God expects us to honor our parents anyway. The Word of God is very clear about this. We all have to admit that it took two parents to bring us into the world... as I see it, God wants to honor them for this. Honoring parents is not based on what they deserve. It is based on honoring God our Father and obeying His directive to honor their office as father and mother.

Also, we have seen demons of death operate through this door to take the person out early. One evening during our Monday deliverance session, a team had a spirit of death manifesting and it wouldn't come out. Back when we first started with deliverance, we would spend a half hour or more trying to drive a demon out. Today, if a spirit does not come out within a few minutes, we call a time out to see if there is still a door open or a legal right for the demon to remain. The team finally discovered the lady was carrying dishonor toward her parents. The woman repented of this and voiced out she now chose to honor her parents. The team was now able to easily cast the spirit out!

"Children, obey your parents in the Lord: for this is right. Honor thy father and mother; which is the first commandment with promise; That it may be well with thee, and thou mayest live long on the earth." (Ephesians 6:1-3)

5) WORKS OF THE FLESH

Galatians 5:19-21 lists the works of the flesh very clearly. This is especially clear when you read the New International Version, since this version gives the works of the flesh in modern English:

"The acts of the sinful nature (works of the flesh) are obvious: sexual immorality, impurity and debauchery; idolatry and witchcraft; hatred, discord, jealousy, fits of rage, selfish ambition, dissentions (divisions), factions and envy; drunkenness, orgies, and the like. I warn you, as I did before, that those who live like this will not inherit the kingdom of God." NIV

(These doors are closed by repenting and asking for forgiveness, which we do in the pre-ministry door-closing prayer).

6) PRIDE

An attitude of pride can be a door we open to a demonic spirit of pride. You will need to mark "pride" on your list and cast it out. The way to close this door is to repent, ask forgiveness for pride and to humble yourself before the Lord.

"Not a novice, lest being lifted up with pride he fall into the condemnation of the devil." (1 Timothy 3:6)

7) WITCHCRAFT

Any involvement with witchcraft will open a door to demonic oppression. Messing with a ouija board, tarot cards, going to a fortune teller, having your palm read, reading horoscopes, astrology, etc. Any time we seek information or powers from anything other than Father God (i.e., witchcraft), a door is opened to serious demonic activity. Years ago "Dungeons and Dragons" was a satanic game that allowed the individual to be demonized... look at all the electronic games with witchcraft overtones today. We have ministered to children who were unable to stay free until Pokémon was taken out of the house. Anything that gives importance to any form of witchcraft is a potential open door to demonic oppression. This gives demons "rights" to torment others in the household and cause weird things to happen in the house. I remember a young lady who did not get free from a spirit of fear until the satanic rock poster was removed from her wall and destroyed. You don't want any sign of any type of witchcraft in your home! This includes any books on witchcraft or the false religions. (See the chapter on exorcising homes, buildings or land).

"There shall not be found among you any one that maketh his son or his daughter to pass through the fire or that useth divination or an observer of times, or an enchanter, or a witch, or a charmer, or a consulter with familiar spirits, or a wizard, or a necromancer. For all that do these things are an abomination unto the Lord: and because of these abominations the Lord thy God doth drive them out from before thee." (Deuteronomy 18:10-12)

8) DRUGS, ALCOHOL AND OTHER ADDICTIONS

Spacing your mind out with addictive drugs is certainly letting your guard down and giving room for demonization. Idolatry can be a factor here also. The addiction can become number one in your life rather than Jesus. The enemy will use addictions as an open door to give evil spirits permission to harass.

9) TRAUMAS OF THE PAST

Most people are carrying emotional wounds of the past, affecting their lives today. There are wounds from bad relationships, rejection (perceived or real), abandonment, physical, verbal, psychological or sexual abuse, severe frightening experiences, experiences with miscarriages, abortions, or having bad childhood memories... these traumas need **inner healing**. Evil spirits will ride in on these wounds. Therefore, you must allow Jesus to heal your heart (see Chapter 7).

"but be ye transformed by the renewing of your mind..." (Romans 12:2). "...He hath sent me to heal the brokenhearted... to set at liberty them that are bruised..." (Luke 4:18).

10) HYPNOSIS

It is dangerous to yield our mind to someone else through hypnosis. We are opening our minds up, and anything could come through that open door when we are under someone else's control. An ungodly soul tie may easily form, which is a door open to the enemy. What if that person is into witchcraft? A spirit of witchcraft may enter to control the individual.

"Know ye not, that to whom ye yield yourselves servants to obey, his servants ye are" (Romans 6:16).

11) IDOLATRY

Jesus is to be number one in our lives. If you have made something else out to be number one; then, that is idolatry. This is a door that evil spirits can come through. Matthew 6:33 tells us we are to, "seek ye first the Kingdom of God, and His righteousness; and all these things will be added unto you." "These things" can represent part of the "abundant life" as long as Jesus is number one. But we can make an idol of self, sports, hobbies, our work, money, people, sex, drugs, alcohol, food, collections, problems, sickness, etc. It may seem like we are worshiping these things like a god. The secret societies such as Free Masonry or Eastern Star and their associated organizations may be a form of idolatry. These are other entries demons use to gain access to your mind, will and emotions or imaginations, and your physical body. "Thou shalt have no other gods before me." (Exodus 20:3)

12) REBELLION AND DISOBEDIENCE TOWARD GOD – NOT KEEPING GOD'S COMMANDMENTS

Most people have had some rebellion and disobedience toward God like this in their lives... many of us have gone through stages. Nevertheless, this is considered sin and needs to be repented of and put under the Blood of Jesus. This is done in the pre-ministry door-closing prayer.

A major point here is that this can also be a **generational curse** from past generations and cause a generational curse for our seed. The types of generational curses could be disease, poverty, early death, destruction, trauma, sorrow and tragedy on our lives; especially if we have experienced any of these. The generational curse needs to be broken out loud ... off of us **and our future generations.** (Deuteronomy 28:15-68).

"And the seed of Israel separated themselves from all strangers, and stood and confessed their sins, and the iniquities of their fathers." (Nehemiah 9:2)

We break this generational curse by voicing out and declaring what Jesus did for us at the Cross. Most Christians have never spoken this out over them and their seed. The Word performs itself when Christians speak it. It does not return void. You can't just sit and read it or hear it, you need to be a doer of the Word (James 1:22) and declare out loud that Jesus has redeemed us and that the curse of the law is now broken off of us and our seed! (This is done in the door-closing prayer). I suggest that you speak to your specific problem, declaring that it is under the curse of the law but that you have been redeemed by Jesus at the Cross. Therefore, you are healed. You have long life. You have abundance, etc. "Christ hath redeemed us from the curse of the law, being made a curse for us: for it is written, "Cursed is everyone that hangeth on a tree" (Galatians 3:13).

13) UNGODLY INHERITANCE

It does not seem fair that you and I can receive curses at conception; however, here are curses that the Bible points out to us:

Exodus 20:5 tells that the iniquity **(sin)** of the fathers as far as **four generations** back can be held against us. It is likely that this four-generation curse would apply to most of us because we have parents and grandparents who have sinned. Involvement with murders, suicides and/or abortions, by us or our forefathers, would certainly fit here. Sins caused by taking certain oaths, speaking and accepting ungodly dedications, or allowing certain secret society curses to be spoken (such as Free Masonry, Eastern Star, etc.) over us typically results in generational demonic activity as well.

There is a generational door (curse) that extends to **ten generations** due to illegitimacies (a baby born out of wedlock) in a family (Deuteronomy 23:2). Think about it. If we figured 40 years to a generation that would be 400 years of ancestors. What are the odds that some of this has taken place? Very high!

The good news is that we can repent of these sins, whether they are known by us or unknown. We can do this for ourselves and on behalf of our forefathers, asking God's forgiveness. And since we have ALL power in Jesus' Name (Luke 10:19), we can break these curses. The breaking of generational curses will be addressed in the door-closing prayer.

"And the seed of Israel separated themselves from all strangers, and stood and confessed their sins, and the iniquities of their fathers." (Nehemiah 9:2)

14) CURSES BY THE TONGUE

"Life and death are in the power of the tongue; and they that love it shall eat the fruit thereof" (Proverbs 18:21). **Certainly, witches** learn this early on in their lives as they are trained to speak curses, spells, incantations, etc. I have encountered generational witchcraft curses on Christians receiving deliverance ministry. These demons have disclosed the person who spoke the curses over the family and gave the demon a legal right to be there. Of course, since we have ALL power in Jesus' Name, we can break these curses, also. (Luke 10:19)

I worked with an individual, a man, who was manifesting demonic activity when he was in my office. The demon identified himself as "Illiteracy." I interrogated this spirit of illiteracy as a prisoner of war. I demanded, "How long have you been here?" It answered back by speaking through the man's mouth, "Five generations." I further inquired, "How did you get in this family line?" It answered, "A curse." I said, "Who spoke the curse?" It finally admitted, "A witch!" So here was a five-generation curse of illiteracy on this family line.

I applied "**ALL**" power in Jesus' name and broke this curse off of this man, breaking the curse off his seed. Then, I commanded the associated spirit (illiteracy) to go to the feet of Jesus for judgment. He coughed it out. (I have a recording of this deliverance session.) A few weeks later, I found out that not only did he change dramatically, but his minor children in grade school had a major turn around. The generational curse was broken.

There is an important point that we need to make here: When someone calls in asking about ministry for their children, I usually ask the parent(s) to go through our ministry first. We want to get the generational curses broken off the parents and their seed before we consider the children. We want to see how the children are doing after the parents' deliverance. It may or may not be necessary to schedule a one-on-one ministry time later.

Can Christians speak curses over someone else or themselves? The same power of the tongue applies to Christians, e**specially Christians.**" The scriptures say, "he shall have whatsoever he saith." (Mark 11:23) So the answer is **YES**. We are encouraged to use our tongue in a positive way to believe and speak God's blessings. Sadly, we have sometimes messed up by the slip of our tongue. As I started learning how the spirit world works ... by the tongue ... I had to do some readjusting. Now, I am careful about speaking negative words because they might become a curse the enemy can use to hurt us.

Here is another case in point. I remember a man I was ministering to during our weekly Monday evening ministry. A demon manifested and gave its name as "Illiteracy." It said, "I have been there three generations." I thought, "Here we go again, another witchcraft curse." But when I demanded to know who spoke the curse, the demon disclosed, "A teacher." A teacher! Yet, you can see how this might happen. Let's say little Johnny has not done well in classroom participation or his homework. The teacher may then get angry saying, "You are stupid, you will never learn anything, (and maybe saying) you are illiterate!" Then, it becomes a curse. In any case, here I am ministering to this man three generations later and that was the source of the curse. A teacher! Of course, I broke the curse with **"ALL"** power again in Jesus' Name and cast out the spirit. (Luke 10:19; Mark 16:17)

15) UNGODLY SOUL TIES

All soul ties form in the same way... good or bad. Soul ties form in our hearts by associating with someone, by bonding, following them, by accepting their influence. These soul ties can be good, and we want to encourage good soul ties. However, these can also be bad or evil soul ties affecting our lives in a very negative way. If you follow a person down an evil kind of path, **un**godly soul ties probably will form. Ungodly soul ties take form from such activities as addictions, drug addiction, alcohol, gambling, stealing, or cult activity. Also, there are secret societies where you declare ungodly dedications, pacts or vows. Some make an idol of someone. Sexual activity outside of marriage will set up ungodly soul ties. Sexual abuse will form an ungodly soul tie, unfair as it is. Additionally, if there has been a lot of strife, fighting, cursing, many hurts, control issues, ungodly soul ties can form with those in our families, with our spouse, our parents, or ex-spouses (See Chapter 6 for more detail). We use a specific prayer to break these ungodly soul ties. (We can do them in a group; however, dealing with them one-on-one is usually the most effective.) A control spirit operating by that person's name who was doing the controlling may need to be renounced and cast out. You need to work up a list of these possible ungodly soul ties. (See the last part of the problem list). Example of godly soul ties: "...the soul of Jonathan was knit with the soul of David, and Jonathan loved him as his own life." (1 Samuel 18:1)

MORE DOORS HAVE BEEN OPENED THROUGH THE OCCULT

Most demons that torment Christians come through doors that they or their ancestors opened. Other demonic spirits are there by a satanic assignment. As discussed before, one of these doors is any involvement with witchcraft through ouija boards, having your palm read, going to a fortune teller, horoscopes, tarot cards, palm readers...the list goes on and on. Any time we seek information from the satanic world or covet objects that represent the dark side, legal rights can be given for demons to enter our soul or physical body. These types of things are "...an abomination unto the Lord." (Deuteronomy 18:10-12)

Children are tormented by demons that came through these doors that were opened to the enemy: Pokémon, dream catchers, unicorns, posters on their walls of satanic rock groups and their music, "Dungeons and Dragons," etc. Any game or book that promotes witchcraft can be a door we open for demonic harassment. Yes, even Harry Potter. I have heard of young people who got so caught up in the "powers" of witchcraft they have gone online pulling up witchcraft web sites to determine the best ways to cast spells. This is the dark side of the supernatural. It is real.

Some years ago, a senior vice president in my mortgage banking company and former naval aviator named Bruce had an interesting experience. He had recently become a born again Christian, and he and his wife had bought an older three-story home here in Oklahoma City. They did some extensive remodeling to the home and added new furniture and paintings. After they moved in, they were hearing noises during the night. Finally, Bruce went into one of the bedrooms. As he opened the closet door, something came out of the closet, knocked him to the floor and wrestled with him, and he could not see it! He finally remembered the Name above all Names and yelled out, "Jesus." The spirit blew off.

After he told me about it, we decided to handle this problem in person. A spirit-filled friend of mine who discerned quite well and I went to his house to blow this thing out of the house. It did not take a lot of discernment at all... there on the wall next to the closet was a large painting of a unicorn! After I explained to him about unicorns, he tore it out of the frame and destroyed it. After destroying the painting, they had no more problems.

We have seen similar situations with children who were being tormented with fear and other torments, including infirmities. When the objects were taken out of the house, they stayed free.

CHAPTER 5

THE PRE-MINISTRY PRAYER (DOOR-CLOSING PRAYER)

THE MINISTER TO LEAD IN WITH THE FOLLOWING:

Jesus, we just thank You again for who You are and what You did for us at the cross. And we put our eyes on You, Jesus. We worship You, we honor You, we glorify You. For Jesus, You are our everything. Thank You, Jesus, that You are our Savior, our Deliverer, our Baptizer and our Healer (physically, mentally, and emotionally). Lord, You are our answer even in the financial world. You are our everything, Jesus. Our eyes are on You. We are reaching out to touch You, Jesus, just like the woman with the issue of blood. She knew if she could just push her way through the crowd and touch You, that Your power would flow. Well, Jesus, here we are, reaching out to You…to touch You. Glory to Your name.

Lord, as You have told us in Your word, we have power over ALL the enemy in Your Name and nothing shall harm us. As we pray, **we declare all of this on a permanent basis** with us and our seed. Now, with this power we address the strongholds of the air that would have any influence or control over the demonic activity in the people (or person) here for ministry. I cancel all assignments that would try to deceive or block successful ministry. We rebuke all demons of the assignments. We call upon God's angels according to Hebrews 1:14 to be of service to the heirs of salvation. Angels, go forth now. Warring angels of the air, cut those strongholds, breaking them off, terminate all gatekeepers and backups, in the Name of Jesus, pulling them down. Angels go forth, in Jesus' Name.

We call upon God's angels at ground level to circle up with us now. Warring angels, we welcome you into this place, swords drawn, ready to help us, to be right with us to protect us in every way, fighting and warring right with us. Thank you, angels ... for being here.

Holy Spirit, we ask You to come and guide us, show us how to pray, anoint us to minister and anoint those who have come that they may receive. We welcome You, Holy Spirit.

Now we speak the protective blood of Christ Jesus over us, our families, our homes, our activities, our ministries, our work, our health, our attitudes, our finances, our possessions, our animals or our pets. The blood of Christ Jesus covers us all. And further, we put every evil spirit on notice; as you come out, you have to go directly to the feet of Jesus for Jesus to do what He wishes with you. I forbid any transference of evil spirits whatsoever. There will be no transferring out and coming back later. One-way traffic, out only. And angels, we call upon you to back these commands and also to mop up at the end of the ministry session, any demonic activity that would linger, in Jesus' Name.

Jesus, as Your Word says, if we seek You, we'll find You.

JUST REPEAT THIS AFTER ME: Jesus, here I am. I'm seeking You. I'm reaching out to You. Set me free, Jesus. I'm tired of the torment and the harassment that's been going on in my life. Set me free, Jesus. I'm ready. Satan, I renounce you and all your demons. And you're bound, Satan. Strongman of my house ... you are bound as well. I put you all on notice now, I follow Jesus. For Jesus, You are the Lord of my life. I'm Yours now. I surrender. I ask You to take over now. You lead me. You guide me. You show me the way. I haven't done that good at it, so You're in charge, Lord, 100 percent. Whatever sin I may have in my life, I confess my sins now. I repent. I ask that You forgive me.

MINISTER AGAIN: Just take a moment now. Let the Holy Spirit just show you, if He's convicting you of any specific sin, now's the time you want to whisper to Him, asking Him to forgive you. Help them, Holy Spirit. (The minister pauses for this.)

PRAY THIS: Thank You, Jesus, for this free gift that washes that sin away. It is not of works but it is a free gift by grace. How awesome You are, Lord. Thank You, Jesus. Thank You, Lord. Thank You for washing this sin away. As the scriptures say, You don't even remember my sin anymore. It's all gone ... a free gift ... thank You, Jesus. I receive my forgiveness.

Jesus, as You have forgiven me, when I really haven't deserved it, I now in turn, choose to forgive all the people who I think have wronged me. I forgive them even though they don't deserve it. As You have done this for me, I do it for them. And Jesus, I do believe that You are the Son of God, that God raised you from the dead and You are Lord. Therefore, by these confessions, and the sincerity of my prayer, I know that I am born again. Hallelujah, thank You, Lord.

MINISTER: You need to consider water baptism if this was your first time to pray this or if you are not sure that you prayed this sincerely in the past.

PRAY THIS TOO: And Jesus, I repent of any involvement with witchcraft, known or unknown for myself and all my generations back. And I renounce any witchcraft powers. I only want the powers of the Holy Spirit.

I repent for not giving; forgive me, Lord.

I repent for any hypnosis, forgive me.

I repent for any idolatry. I confess this as a sin, Lord, generational or otherwise. I put my eyes on You now, Jesus. You are number one in my life.

I repent of any dishonor that I carry toward my parents. Forgive me, Lord, for I put aside the things that may have happened between my parents and me. …. In obedience to Your Word, Lord, I forgive them and I choose now to honor them.

I repent of any illegitimacy that is present in my family lines, … for all generations back. I ask that You forgive us, Lord. And therefore, in Jesus' name, I break the curse of illegitimacy off of my seed and me.

I repent of having received fear into my life. Forgive me Lord, for I am learning. I'm beginning to see how fear is the opposite of faith. So I choose now to stand on Your Word, Lord, to stand in faith. Therefore, I renounce and I rebuke all fear.

I repent for pride, forgive me, Lord, for I humble myself before You.

I repent for the works of the flesh, of sexual immorality, or drunkenness, or drugs, addictions, jealousy, envy, anger, rage, fighting. Forgive me, Lord.

I repent for rebellion and disobedience that I've had toward You, God, on behalf of my ancestors and me. I confess this as a sin. Therefore, by the word in Galatians 3:13, Jesus has redeemed me from the curse of the law. I declare this now. I break the curse of the law off of my family, my seed and me.

I repent for having spoken any curses upon others, or myself. I repent of any ungodly vows that I may have spoken over myself, even from years ago. For if I have done this, I ask that You forgive me, Lord. I cancel them in Jesus' Name. And I renounce and I rebuke all related demons.

I repent of the sins of my forefathers, for all generations back. I forgive them, and I ask that You too, forgive them, Lord. And therefore, by the Blood of Jesus, I break the power of all generational curses, spells, inherited spirits of Satan, and spirits of infirmity. I break them off of myself and my future generations. I sever, in Jesus' Name, any satanic generational or self-spoken contracts, vows, dedications, pacts, oaths, ties, programs, seals and assignments. I especially cancel all assignments against me, to lie to my mind, to try to influence me to walk down the wrong path. I cancel these lies now, permanently, in Jesus' name. I declare that from this time forth, I will only listen to the truth and the voice of my Jesus and the Holy Spirit. I also cancel all assignments that would influence the demons in the people around me to my detriment, in Jesus' Name.

I repent of any involvement with secret societies, Free Masonry, Eastern Star and their associated organizations. On behalf of myself and my ancestors, I confess this as a sin. I ask that You forgive us. Therefore, in Jesus' Name, I break any related curses off my family, my seed and me.

I cancel all satanic prayers or incantations that have been prayed over me and my family, any hexes, vexes, voodoo, Indian curses, medicine man curses, curses upon the land where I live or my home, objects within my home, my possessions, including my animals or my pets.

I cancel, in Jesus' Name, all genetic and DNA defects. I command my genetics and my DNA to line up now with my inheritance in Christ Jesus.

I cancel all psychic activity and all ungodly soul ties, including any witchcraft generational soul ties that may exist between others, myself and my seed. I rebuke all related demon control spirits. I also call back any fragmented pieces of my soul and for my soul to be made whole and reseated in proper order and balance as God designed it to be.

I proclaim my freedom by the blood of Jesus, the freedom of my family and of my seed, in Jesus' Name. It is done! Thank You, Lord, for the power that is in Your name. Thank You, Lord. Thank You, Jesus.

Jesus, since You have forgiven me, and I know that You have, I now, in turn, forgive myself. I put aside all the things that have happened, including things that I think I should have done or didn't do. I know I'm forgiven … my sin is not even remembered anymore. I know that the Father sent His Son to the cross just for me. Since He did all that, yes, I can forgive myself. So I do it. It's done. It's behind me.

If my heart's been broken, I forgive the one who has done this. Holy Spirit, I ask that You wash my broken heart now, with the precious blood of Jesus … cleansing it, mending it, healing it, making my heart new again. I receive a new heart and a new start. And if I carry bags of bruises, and hurts, and emotional pain, I don't want the load of them anymore. Jesus, I cast my cares upon You. So I'm taking this load, all these hurts, emotional pain, all these bags of bruises, I'm pulling them out Lord, I'm giving them to You.

MINISTER: Pull them out. Just take your hand and pull them out and hand them up to Jesus. He's ready to take them if you'll give them to Him.

PRAY THIS: Thank You, Jesus. Thank You, Lord, for taking them. Thank You, Jesus. Thank You, Lord. Lord, You're sure stronger than us. Thank You that You're there. Thank You, Jesus. Thank You, Lord.

God, if I have blamed You for things that have happened, I'm sorry, forgive me. For I am still learning that it is Satan who comes to steal, kill, and destroy, but that You have come, Jesus, that I might have life, abundant life (see John 10:10) and blessings. I choose You, Jesus, life and blessings.

Now, Holy Spirit, I've already committed to forgive all the people who I think have wronged me or offended me. But if there's any resentment, bitterness, emotional pain, rejection, feelings of betrayal, neglect, abandonment … show me who that's with. I'll be obedient. I'll release them to you, Jesus. I'll forgive them.

MINISTER: Just let the Holy Spirit work with you now. He's already starting to put names and faces into your mind. Let Him take you through your family, your friends, places you've worked, school days, churches you've been in where there are hurt feelings, help them, Holy Spirit, just help them, in Jesus' Name. Just keep working on this. Take all the time you need. You don't want one ounce of unforgiveness left in your life.

God's angels, circle around us. Thank You, Lord, that You are working with us, that Your Word is performing itself with supernatural signs following. I declare this place to be holy ground.

(ALLOW THE PERSON OR PEOPLE PLENTY OF TIME FOR THE HOLY SPIRIT TO SHOW THEM THOSE THEY NEED TO FORGIVE.)

CHAPTER 6

BREAKING UNGODLY SOUL TIES

One of the primary areas of ministry we do is breaking ungodly (or demonic) soul ties. Many people get so much relief and feel so good from this type of ministry that they think they are finished. We are often surprised to find out later that a certain number of problems the person marked on their problem list disappeared as we broke off the ungodly soul ties and commanded the control spirit and other associated spirits to leave.

So, how do "ungodly soul ties" develop? The same way godly soul ties develop ... by associating with someone and by bonding with them. We read about godly soul ties in 1 Samuel 18:1, "that the soul of Jonathan was knit with the soul of David, and Jonathan loved him as his own soul."

Since Satan seems to have a counterfeit for what God has for us, ungodly soul ties tend to develop from any shared intimacy outside of the norm; i.e., outside of what God has ordained. This is especially true if you associate and bond with someone who leads you down an ungodly path, such as drugs, alcohol, sex outside marriage, homosexuality, pornography, the occult, a cult, and other sin. When a person has been victimized sexually, unfair as it is to the victim, an ungodly soul tie formed that needs to be broken. Many have been sexually abused by a parent or relative or someone close to the family.

In the prayer model that we use, we break the ungodly soul ties and we choose to leave the godly soul ties. I think it is important to understand that we want godly relationships; especially when this involves a parent or a relative. You are keeping the good soul ties that exist.

In this day and time, we minister to many individuals who have had numerous sexual encounters. I remember a man who came to the Monday evening deliverance meeting. After I taught about the soul ties and how sex outside of marriage was a problem, I noticed he wrote down two long lists of names on a blank piece of paper. I was amazed that he could remember each of their names! I could also see that there was no way I would be able to take him through the prayer model one at a time when I was ministering to him. It would take all night to accomplish that! So, I just called it the "sexual group," and went through the prayer ... it seemed to work just fine. When there is a group like this, there may be one or two important relationships that you might want to name individually, instead of including them in that group.

After the breaking ungodly soul ties prayer, I like to ask the Holy Spirit to bring back fragmented pieces of the person's soul, to make their soul whole again. This is especially important because of the sexual activity outside of marriage. It is quite possible that in each sexual encounter, or experience outside of marriage, or with an ex-spouse, a portion of the person's soul was fragmented off because of the "one flesh" concept in scripture. (Matt. 19:5; Mark 10:8; 1 Cor. 6:16 and Eph. 5:31)

This prayer is especially helpful if a parent or anyone whom the candidates for ministry know or work with has been very controlling in their lives. I look at it this way: there is no downside to prayer. We terminate any bad soul ties and you keep the good ones.

An ex-spouse is always a candidate for this prayer because of the sexual relationship and the strife that comes from a marriage break-up. Curses may have been spoken that need to be broken.

For married partners, especially if there are marriage problems, it is quite possible that an ungodly soul tie may have developed between the spouses. I have seen great results when only one of the spouses has prayed the soul tie prayer.

Strange as it might sound, there can be ungodly soul ties with animals. A bad relationship with pets that are not doing what you expect of them will create an ungodly soul tie. Of course, bestiality (sexual involvement with an animal) would cause a demonic soul tie to form. An out-of-balance relationship, especially making the pet an idol, would be suspicious ... dolls, stuffed animals, an object, a book, a computer (especially if something like pornography was involved) can become an idol in a person's life.

Summing up, ungodly soul ties seem to develop through:
- Sex outside of marriage
- Sexual involvement with demons (succubus or incubus)
- Ex-spouses, present spouse, sexual relationships
- Abuse of any kind (especially sexually)
- Following someone into a cult, witchcraft or false religion
- Following someone down a path of alcohol, drugs, pornography, etc.
- Spoken curses over you
- Physical, mental or emotional hurt
- Strange, out-of-balance or negative control over you
- Parents and siblings may develop ungodly soul ties through life experiences
- I often put similar groups together such as a sexual group, etc.

Here is the prayer model I like to use, have the person say the following:

Jesus, I forgive (the name or names) for all that has happened, for all that has gone on. I forgive him/her/or them. I choose to bless them. I repent of any sin that I have committed in these relationships. Forgive me, Lord. I forgive myself. I now put (the name, names or group) into my hands (cup your hands), as well as any bad or tormenting feelings and unforgiveness that I yet carry toward (the name). Any hurts, bitterness, anger, resentment, betrayal, rejection, sadness, disappointment, offense, neglect, feelings of abandonment, deception, lies, criticism, manipulation, and control. (Ask the person to name off others. Look at the suspect list for possible others.)

Jesus, I'm tired of carrying this load, so I'm handing (the name) over to You for You to see after him/her and I am giving You all these tormenting feelings, in Jesus' Name ... I'm cleaning my house, Lord, so here they are, Lord, I give them to You. (Tell the person to now lift up his hands...to just see Jesus reaching down and taking them. If you give them, Jesus will take them every time. (1 Peter 5:7, "casting all our cares upon him, for He cares for us.")

In Jesus' Name, I break the power of any curses that (the name) may have spoken over me (I sometimes add, I don't believe that he/she would have meant to, but if it happened by the slip of his/her tongue, then I break them). I also rescind any curses that I may have spoken over him/her or myself. (If a parent, break generational curses) I cancel any ungodly vows that I may have made. I break all these off of me and terminate all ungodly soul ties. (I keep the godly soul ties.) I break these spiritually, physically, mentally, emotionally, and financially. (And sexually if it applies.)

Now, I command any evil spirits that came through these soul ties to go to the feet of Jesus for judgment. Control spirits coming through (name the individual(s)), any associated demons of the curses or vows, all related spirits, to circle up together and go to the feet of Jesus. In Jesus' Name, now GO! Demons of the curses, in the Name of Jesus, GO! (Engage now and stay on the offense until you feel they are all gone) With the Bible, touch areas where you may feel the spirits moving in your body, as led.

Inner-healing in this relationship.

Jesus, come, put Your arms around _____ (name) as Your child, to comfort, to reassure the person, to love, to talk with them. **Speak Your truth** concerning this (or those) relationship(s), so that any lies that were thought to be a truth can be clarified. [Wait until Jesus is finished with the person. It may take only a minute or several minutes. Don't rush it.]

I am constantly amazed how often people will hear Jesus share with them a clear truth about that relationship when we do this inner healing at the end of the soul tie prayer. A wonderful healing comes about when Jesus speaks to us with **His truth**. If the person was able to hear Jesus and is able to report what He said, I like to ask, "Can you accept what He said as the truth?" The answer seems to always be "yes."

Some people don't hear Jesus speak to them. They seem to always experience a supernatural peace that was not there before and the tormenting feelings concerning that person(s) are greatly reduced, or completely gone. I am convinced that when we ask Jesus to speak to us. He does. When we are not sensitive enough to actually hear Him, He speaks into our spirit man. **Healing comes when Jesus speaks.**

CHAPTER 7

DOING INNER HEALING OF PAST WOUNDS

Our Jesus is a total healer. He heals us in our spirits when we are born again. He also heals us physically, mentally, emotionally, financially, and sexually as it may apply.

In Luke 4:18, Jesus said, "The Spirit of the Lord is upon me, because he hath anointed me to preach the gospel to the poor; he hath sent me to heal the broken hearted, to preach deliverance to the captives, and recovery of sight to the blind, to set at liberty them that are bruised."

Many Christians still carry wounds and stressful, tormenting memories of events from the past. These affect them in their day-to-day living more than they realize! These stressful mental and emotional wounds can be an entry for tormenting evil spirits. Inner healing is needed to deal with these wounds. In fact, this is a MUST to have easy and lasting deliverance and/or physical healing. We have learned it is best to spend as much time as necessary doing inner healing to have lasting results.

The Word tells us in Romans 12:2 to be "transformed by the renewing of your mind." Jesus is ready to deal with this renewing of our minds if we will put our eyes on Him and let Him heal us through the ministry of the Holy Spirit.

There are many ways to do inner healing ... here is one of the simple methods that any Christian can quickly learn to do to help the hurting people around them:

When I first sit down with people, I look over their problem list and ask them what they feel is their main area of concern. What is tormenting them the most? What would they like to accomplish most out of the ministry time? (If the person has not filled out their problem list, these questions are still a good initial lead-in to start developing an understanding of their need for inner healing).

I ask them about their childhood: Was there sexual abuse? Rejection? Neglect? Abandonment? Severe frightening experiences? Do they have feelings of betrayal? Deep bitterness? Have they experienced other traumas?

Most people need at least some inner healing concerning the loss of loved ones. If they have lost a child, I can assure you that they will need this type of ministry. We cannot overlook miscarriages or involvements with abortions (the one who experienced the abortion, those who took the woman, and those who paid for it). Repentance and/or self-forgiveness may be needed.

When it is time to minister concerning the loss of loved ones, I usually have the person cup their hands and say something like this: "Lord, this is hard for me, but I know it is time for me to do this, it's time for my closure ... so, Jesus, I'm putting (baby or person) into my hands to give to You now, for You to care for. As You gave this baby (or name of baby or name of person) to me, I give this baby (or name of person) unto You."

I ask the people to lift their hands up to Jesus and ask them to try to envision Jesus reaching down and lifting the child or person right out of their hands. If they can't see Jesus, just tell them that is okay ... Jesus is always ready to take them if we will give them to Him. (1 Peter 5:7 "Cast our cares upon Him.")

Then, I ask Jesus (the Holy Spirit revealing Jesus) to show the person others who need to be released. It's usually best, I believe, to do this releasing to Jesus one at a time, if time allows.

If, from my interview with the person, I feel they have a lot of condemnation, abandonment, unworthiness, rejection, self-rejection, or rejection in the womb, then I know that they probably need inner healing from conception, so they clearly see that their birth was not an accident.

To do this, I ask Jesus (the Holy Spirit revealing Jesus) to take the person back to the womb when the father's sperm was seeking the mother's egg. I ask the person to envision that Jesus was there, directing the father's sperm, a particular sperm, a very special sperm to the mother's egg ... conception has now taken place! This person was no accident and was conceived with special gifts and talents.

Now, I ask them to allow the Holy Spirit to take them back to the first month in the womb ... how is their life, baby (<u>name of person</u>) this first month? What feelings can they detect? (Some people describe very clearly, month by month, what was going on, both inside and outside the womb and their associated feelings.)

Whenever I notice that they have locked onto a bad memory with tormenting, negative feelings and emotions (i.e., fear, rejection, hurt, pain, bitterness, anger, stress, depression, abandonment), I start the inner healing process. I usually ask at this point, "Can you feel these bad feelings inside somewhere?" Most people report, "In my belly area." Then I say, "believe that you have a spiritual hand that can go right into your belly and can take hold of those balled up, tormenting feelings, as well as any satanic lies that may be perceived as a truth ... take hold of them, pull them out and hand them up to Jesus."

A number of people report that they see Jesus right there in the womb with them. I often ask Jesus to go over and to put His arms around baby (<u>the person's name</u>), to comfort, to love, to give security, strength, to just hold, to hug, to talk with and to reveal His truth so this tormenting memory can be healed. Then I continue through each month in the womb until birth, giving the Holy Spirit an opportunity to bring inner healing.

I ask them to see themselves at birth now. As they are born, Jesus is there. He reaches down with a towel, a big smile on His face, and picks up baby (<u>name</u>). "You have arrived! Jesus is proud and excited that you are now here with your special gifts and talents."

Now I ask Jesus (the Holy Spirit revealing Jesus) to show the people their life in the first year. I ask Jesus to hold them and speak truth to them, doing inner healing again as they become aware of more bad memories and the associated feelings. Then, the next year, etc. With the majority of people I minister to, I don't feel led to go all the way back to the womb. Rather, I just ask the Holy Spirit to take them back to birth. Then, I ask the Holy Spirit to take them from birth through their life's experiences to today, stopping them on a trauma or memory that needs healing. I ask the Holy Spirit to show the person that these events are possible roots or entries that evil spirits have used, including spirits of infirmity.

Remember, when this person sees an event or locks onto a bad memory or picture, I ask them to describe how this makes them feel.

As the minister, I find that I don't have to know details of the trauma. Rather, I need to know the feelings that they can identify as the person sees themselves in that memory. After the bad feelings are identified, I ask them to take that spiritual hand and go inside (again, they often feel those feelings in their belly or chest area), to get their hand around those balled-up, tormenting feelings, those satanic lies, pull them out and hand them up to Jesus. "Just see Jesus reaching down and taking them all out of their hands." Once I see that they have accomplished this task, I confirm with the person that they saw or felt Jesus take them. I have found that when the person will give them to Jesus, Jesus will take them!

At this point, I like to ask them, "Can you see Jesus anywhere there with you?" Most people will be able to see Jesus there with them and what He is doing. Many times, He will have His arms out to them. I normally say, "Run over to Him and let Jesus hold you ... and hug you." If they can't see Jesus, I just ask Jesus to go to them, to hold them and hug them, to talk to them, sharing His truth about that event.

I then say to the people: "As He holds you, just bask in that love, that strength, that comfort, that peace, that security. **ASK JESUS TO REVEAL**

HIS TRUTH replacing all those lies you may have accepted. <u>Let Jesus talk with you as long as necessary</u>. Let Him tell you whatever He wants you to know about the situation." (I give them a minute or so. ... With some people it takes longer ... keep tissue handy.) When they are finished, I ask the Lord to show the individual another trauma or tormenting picture that needs healing, and go through the same process until there are no more wounds that need healing.

We may focus on only a few events during their lifetime, or quite a few. Usually we will hit on the major inner healing need that has been an entry for the spirits of sickness and other demonic activity. Once we complete the inner healing process, we have normally dealt with most of the doorways to demonic activity.

CHAPTER 8

HOW TO MINISTER TO YOURSELF AND OTHERS

ENGAGING AND CASTING OUT EVIL SPIRITS

Once you have learned about the spiritual war that you are in, how important it is to deal with the roots of the demons by the 15-minute pre-ministry prayer (door-closing prayer), followed by breaking the ungodly soul ties and inner healing; then casting the demons out is typically very easy. Often, a certain number of demons will leave as these three steps are accomplished. Remember, this order of ministry is not written in stone, but it does work rather well, most of the time. Let the Holy Spirit lead you.

On occasion, you may need to bind evil spirits or command the demons to be still in order to get the person through the steps of closing the doors, breaking the ungodly soul ties and inner healing. Because there may be a manifestation of demonic activity that is attempting to keep you from completing these steps, you may have to speak to the demon and say, "Be silent," so that you can proceed. If a demon has taken over, bind the spirit and call the person by name to come up, to fight their way to the surface and to stay, in Jesus Name.

As you begin to repent and renounce each spirit on the problem list, it normally takes less than a minute per demon or demon group to get rid of them. If it takes longer than this, there may still be some roots to demonic oppression that have not been severed or dealt with completely ... often there is still unforgiveness, un-repented sin, or some curse that has been missed. Often we discover that there are assignments that need to be broken.

The Holy Spirit will usually disclose whatever is necessary for ministry when He is asked. (Sometimes people have the gift of the Spirit called the discerning of spirits. You can ask for this gift from the Holy Spirit. However, we can minister effectively even when we don't have this gift.) When you are commanding the spirits to leave, sometimes a demon will confess the specifics of its remaining rights to oppress as you interrogate it. I have had demons disclose that there is a generational curse that has not been broken. I prefer to put the demon on standby and call the person back up so that they would use their own voice to break the generational curse because they are living representatives of the family line. Or, the minister could just break the curse himself. (See the techniques in the Head Demon chapter 9).

Since most of the people feel the demons being cast out, you just stay in the attack mode until that particular spirit, or group of spirits is gone. I like to quote Luke 10:19 often. It is good to declare that we have all power (in His name) over the enemy and nothing shall by any means hurt us. The demons hate to hear Christians quote this. (It's nice for us to torment them for a change.)

I start looking over the problem list as I ask the Holy Spirit to show me how to pray. The Holy Spirit seems to give me direction on which spirit suspects to address first. I usually address more than what they might mark on the list. The bitterness group, death group, destroyer group, deception, rejection, condemnation, and heaviness are groups I usually address. In fact, we have made it easy by identifying those groups I usually address with people by using an * (asterisk).

A technique that can work rather well is to ask the person what they think is their major concern on their problem list (like anger, bitterness, depression, stress, anxiety, addictions, etc.). Then ask Jesus to take them back to the earliest root or source of this particular problem area. Just wait while Jesus shows them a scene or event. (Often, Jesus will take them back into a childhood experience.) As they lock onto something, it is time to do inner healing if they have not already covered this event. I ask them to identify the feelings and emotions associated with the event or trauma. Some people can feel these feelings and/or emotions balled up in their stomach or chest. If so, I ask them to use their hand as a spiritual hand, place their spiritual hand inside their stomach or chest, and get hold of those balled-up feelings and/or emotions. Pull them out and hand them up to Jesus. Then, I ask Jesus to talk to them, to comfort them and love on them, speaking His truth about the situation. I don't hurry this process. I tell them to wait while Jesus speaks His truth to their heart. If they can't hear Jesus, I just tell them that I believe He spoke truth to their spirit man. Let the peace of God rest on them in this process.

As they focus on a particular suspect that is on their problem list, I make sure they determine to repent and renounce this problem area. I ask them to speak this out loud, choosing to engage their spirit man, "Jesus, I repent for carrying (for example) bitterness, hatred, self-hate, unforgiveness, hurt, resentment, jealousy. Forgive me, Lord."

Now I command bitterness (or whatever name of spirit I am commanding to leave) and all related spirits to circle and bind up together ... go to the feet of Jesus for judgment. In Jesus' Name, go!! By the Blood of Jesus … let go. In Jesus' Name, go…go…keep going…by the blood. (I keep commanding until they experience relief or they feel that it is gone. I often suggest taking a deep breath and expel anything out that is in there. When I cast out a demon, they expel the demon. They blow it out.)

If they are feeling the demon moving, or it is painful, I touch the Bible on the spot so that it can keep it moving on out. Often, the evil spirit might move out of the stomach area and upward toward the throat. As it comes into the throat, some people will yawn them out, some cough them out, and others burp them out. I take a pen and mark off that particular demonic group from the list.

Then I go to the next problem on the list or group as the Holy Spirit leads.

There is a small percentage of people that we minister to who do not seem to feel or hear anything. However, if we proceed by faith, we find out later that they are just as free as the person who experienced a lot during the deliverance. I have had to conclude that there are some Christians who are just not very sensitive to the spirit world. The Word still performs itself as we Christians speak it.

Early in this ministry, in the late 70s or early 80s, a pastor in Arkansas shared with me that evil spirits not only don't want to hear the Word quoted, but they detest the physical Word. He told me that when someone is feeling a demon moving around inside their body and when it does not seem to be coming out … take the Bible and touch it on the spot where they feel the spirit. The demon will run from the Word. I started trying this in ministry sessions and found it really worked well.

Sometimes there is delayed deliverance. This seems to be quite common with children. Parents report that a week or two passes before any changes take place in the children. Sometimes adults experience this also. I remember a lady who said she did not feel anything the evening she received ministry, but several weeks later she was lying on her couch and the spirits suddenly came "bubbling up out of her." Then she was free.

We see the same delay sometimes with physical healings. While healing is often immediate, especially with backs, it may be a few days or even months before a person experiences healing. Of course, sin and/or unforgiveness toward others or ourselves will block deliverance or healing. Many times I have seen immediate healing experienced when people kept on forgiving until they completed the process.

PRAYING FOR SOMEONE AT DISTANCE

Many people have loved ones, friends, or associates who they believe are being bothered by demonic activity. But those people are not seeking help and probably do not even know about this type of ministry. You can help them, preparing the way in the spirit realm so that they reach out for someone to minister to them (including salvation). I recommend that you use this procedure of praying on a <u>daily</u> basis. (From the privacy of your prayer closet):

STEP 1: Cancel all satanic assignments put on this person, in Jesus' Name and command all demons of the assignments to go to the feet of Jesus.

STEP 2: Decide on a list of problems (see the problem list) you believe they are experiencing. These problems may be the names of actual spirits that are tormenting them. You will find that there will probably be a dozen or more problems on the list. Make sure to take time and forgive the people you are concerned about and bless them in every area you can think of to better release the love of God for them. Then, lift them up in prayer, commanding the blinders to come off their eyes, asking God to intervene. Then, begin to declare things that are not as though they are. Activate the God kind of faith by binding these possible spirits, one at a time; i.e., command each one to be still, not to manifest, not to speak or influence the person you are praying for. Open a spiritual lock box and command these spirits to go into the lock box and be gagged, "In Jesus' Name, I open a spiritual lock box, I command these spirits to go into that lock box and I gag you by the power of the Holy Spirit." It is very important that you do not attempt to cast these spirits out at this point, because the person probably has doors that need to be closed first. You are hoping the person will finally say, "I think I need help." It would be especially exciting if the person would say, "Jesus, help me." The goal is that the individual will get with a minister who understands deliverance, get the doors closed so that ministry can be efficient and lasting.

STEP 3: Now ask Jesus to reveal Himself to the person, to comfort them, to hug as His children and to talk to them, speaking His truth to them about the gospel and who He is, pointing out any lies that the person might have bought into.

STEP 4: Declare God's blessings over them.

CHAPTER 9

HEAD DEMON TECHNIQUE

In 1999, I received a prophecy from Eileen Fisher of Denver, Colorado. She said that the Lord would shortly be showing me a new technique that would bring additional efficiency and speed to the deliverance process. Not long after this, a friend of mine who lived in Connecticut told me about a ministry that was using a technique in which the head demon was called up and used as a "prisoner of war" to gain intelligence on the demonic structure within the person receiving ministry. We use this information to cancel any remaining right the spirits may have. After all the lower ranking spirits are gone, the head demon finally is cast out.

Previously I would get a head demon to manifest, I would try to find out if it had any legal rights remaining, deal with those rights, and cast out the spirit. Then going on to the next demon, finding out its legal rights remaining, if any, canceling those rights and casting it out along with any associated evil spirits. When no more demons surfaced, we concluded the deliverance.

As I started using this head demon technique, I found it **would work on about a third of the people**. It seemed to vary with each person. Some would go into a full manifestation while others would just hear the demons and report what they were hearing. **If I cannot get a good communication flow working, then I just do the usual basic deliverance method of working the problem list.**

I still led the person in the **door-closing prayer**, worked the **soul ties** that needed to be broken, and ministered **inner healing** as necessary, so that the demons would be undermined and weakened. But instead of doing the **problem list,** I would try to call up the head demon or the strongman. Interesting note: If you can get this method to work, it often will show how vicious the demon is toward the person, as well as the demonic devices employed. However, this clearly demonstrates the greater power we Christians have in speaking in His name, the Name of Jesus, and how God's angels are ready to help us if we will ask them to do so.

So, rather than just working the problem list as a part of basic deliverance, have a yellow tablet handy. Tell the person to whom you are ministering to put himself in neutral as much as he can… trying not to think but just speak out anything that comes to him…odd as it might seem.

At this point, I like to quote **Luke 10:19**, i.e., that in the name of Jesus we have **ALL power** over the demonic realm and **nothing shall harm us**. I call upon God's angels to circle up closer around us, to draw their swords and to be ready to discipline these demons as necessary in the event that they do not cooperate. (Hebrews 1:14 – God's angels are available to be of service to the heirs of salvation.)

Then I **command the highest-ranking evil spirit present in the person to come up** from where it is hiding…to come up front and center of the person's mind.

It may take a number of commands. I usually ask the angels to take the tips of their swords and prod the head demon up. Often this will work. The individual either will be hearing what the demon is saying and is able to relay to you as the minister, OR the demon comes up into a full manifestation. **If a clear line of communication is not established, then I just go ahead and do basic deliverance by working the problem list as the Holy Spirit leads.** Remember, this technique seems to work on only about 1/3 of the people. Some people are just not very sensitive to the spirit world.

If I am able to get the head demon up, I like to intimidate it and its group by asking, "Can you see God's angels circled up around us?" Sometimes the demon will use the person's eyes through the manifestation and will begin looking around. The demon will often report that it sees around 8-10 warring angels with their swords drawn…sometimes more. Then I say, "Do you understand the angels are circled up with their swords and are ready to discipline you in the event that you do not cooperate, do not tell the truth, or if you are not quick and clear with your answers? Is this understood?" As soon as it answers yes, I continue.

I like to ask it, "Are there are any demons of equal rank or higher rank than you?" Sometimes, a lower-ranking spirit initially will come up, rather than the highest-ranking spirit. (Which, by the way, also can be helpful. A lower-ranking spirit usually can be interrogated also. Many times, he can be forced to disclose the head demon.)

Because demons are inherent liars it is important to confirm the information they provide by saying, **"Will you confess what you just told me to be true before the Lord Jesus Christ and the Holy Spirit?"** They will answer yes or no to this. If I catch the demon lying, I call upon the angels to initially take their swords and jab the demon three hard times. Many times, you then will see the person jerk three times with the manifestation as they sit in the chair. It's awesome to see the Lord and His angels working right with us on the front lines with these supernatural signs following. (Mark 16:20; Hebrews 1:14)

The more I catch the demon lying through the deliverance, the more severe I get with the use of the angels...jabbing five times, seven times, even severing a spiritual arm or leg as necessary. Most of the time, the demons straighten up after the initial jabs.

Demons are legalistic and military in ranking. By interrogating the head demon you can obtain information regarding the demonic structure of control and oppression. There is normally a head demon in charge with lower ranking department heads that report to him. Those department heads normally have several evil spirits in their group.

Next, I command the head demon, "Reveal how many demons are in your immediate group, in Jesus' Name." Often there will be five or ten, occasionally more that are directly hooked up with the head demon. Additionally I ask, "Do you and your immediate group have any legal rights remaining that have not been revealed to me? Are there any legal rights yet with any of the demons that are in this person? Are there any satanic assignments that have not been broken?" If so, break them and confirm that it is accomplished..

I now interrogate the head demon as to who are its main group leaders. If it answers, for example, one of them is fear, I command, "How many demons are in the fear group?" It might answer, say, eight. Then I command to know, "Does fear and its group of eight have any legal rights to remain or to return?" If it answers yes, I command to know, "What are those rights?" As I find out what those rights are, then I proceed to break those rights, confirming with the head demon that the rights are now broken.

If those rights involve something the person himself needs to do to break it, such as repenting and forgiving, I put the demon on standby and call the person back up to the surface. It may take several commands for the person to come up. Once up, I say, "John Doe, can you hear what the demon is saying?" Around 90% of the people can hear what is going on while 10% cannot hear anything and have to be told what the demon said. I prefer the person to hear, since I don't have to explain everything. Once I feel the right is broken, I call the head demon back up and confirm. Typically, the head demon will disclose all of the group leaders this way so you can follow the same procedure in the paragraphs above.

I like to use the problem list as a guide in interrogating the head demon if I am suspicious about demons that I think may be there in the person but have not yet been disclosed. The head demon will sometimes answer that a certain demon is under a particular group leader. Of course, you would want to confirm that statement. It's always important to command to know what satanic death grips are present in the person. What are they and where are they in the body? Are they activated or inactivated?

You may discover there is a disease (such as cancer) that is present that is not activated yet. Are there any legal rights such as generation curses? Satanic assignments? If there are, then proceed and deal with them...confirming with the head demon that they are broken. Be sure you marked the death grip demons on the yellow tablet to cast out. You can cast them out now or later. Be sure and confirm that they are gone by checking with the head demon again.

Command to know if there is a gatekeeper present, generational or otherwise. If so, mark it down also on the yellow tablet. (Often the head demon is the gatekeeper) Break the gatekeeper rights or assignment and confirm. Are there any back-up programs in place for the demons to return to the person?

Once you have reconfirmed that there are no other evil spirits that have not been disclosed and no remaining legal rights or assignments, I now proceed to take authority over several groups and their associated demons on the yellow tablet and then send them to the feet of Jesus for Jesus to deal with them. Confirm each time with the head demon that they are gone. Then taking authority over another group the same way.

Finally, confirm with the head demon that he is the only demon left, except maybe his immediate helpers, which should be bound up to him. On occasion when rushed for time, I have had the head demon bind all demons that are under its authority up to itself (Including any demons that are attached to any alters or protectors — see below), finally sending them all out together to the feet of Jesus. Be sure to confirm with the head demon that they are all bound up to him and that they stay bound.

If you suspect that there has been abuse, especially sexual abuse, it is very likely there will be some alters, multiple personalities or protectors present. The head demon will often disclose this when commanded. **A true alter (alternate personality) or protector is not a demon,** even though it is quite common to find there are false alters that act like an alter but are actually a demon. It is difficult sometimes to determine if you are speaking to a demon or a true alter. Then there can be alters who are tormented with demons themselves.

One way to determine if you are speaking to a demon or an alter is to use 1 John 4:2 by asking: "Will you confess that Jesus Christ has come in the flesh?" You can also ask them, "Who is your master? Who do you serve?" Sometimes the false alter will immediately admit that it is a demon when asked. I go ahead and terminate its assignment and cast it out once it has been identified as a demon. A true alter is a God-given protector that has been present to enable the person to cope during the abuse. As God heals the memories and emotions/feelings of the person through inner healing, those alters, once born again, can be integrated into the white light of the Holy Spirit. (See the section on "True Multiple Personalities are not demons")

I like to do the ungodly soul ties, the inner healing and cast out the evil spirits first as much as possible, then deal with the alters/protectors last and their integration. This includes having the head demon bind up to himself any demons with the alters or protectors, and to keep them there until they are all sent out to the feet of Jesus.

If the person has been a victim of satanic ritual abuse (SRA), it is best to call in a minister who is seasoned in this and is aware of how to break off the satanic dedications, special programs, devices, seals and satanic blood baptisms.

This is a good time to inquire of the head demon, "What lies have you been speaking into this person's mind?" I often command of the head demon, "Give me the top ten lies that you have been speaking into this person's head." Write them down on the yellow tablet. I then like to ask, "Has he or she been buying into these lies?" The answers from the demon vary. Sometimes the demon reports, "Yes, this person is a pushover." Other times, "No." It seems to depend on how much the person is standing on the Word of God. Now cancel this lie program permanently and rebuke the demons of the lies in Jesus' Name.

Here comes the fun part...command the head demon to stick its head into the storehouse within the person that holds their God-given gifts. Command the demon to name those gifts. Write them down on the tablet. Remember to check these answers with question, "Do you confess these to be true before the Lord Jesus and the Holy Spirit?" Often there will be five to ten, sometimes more. The head demon hates to do this – you may have to use the angels to prod it with their swords. Once the gifts are written down, I like to say, "Is this why you have tried to block this person so much with your lies and demons?" It will always answer yes.

One more final question for the head demon, before sending it and any remaining demons out to the feet of Jesus. Especially if you think there has been some sexual abuse: "Are there any false alters or protectors present?" Are there any demons attached to any alters or protectors?" If so, cancel their assignments and make sure the head demon has bound those up to him as well. Confirm this. The head demon often will also disclose how many true alters or protectors are present, if any. Again, I like to do the deliverance first as much as possible, then deal with the alters or protectors last and their integration.

It is now time to dispose of the head demon and any remaining demons... bind them all up together. **Confirm** this is done with the head demon. **Now have the head demon repeat the following: "Before the Lord Jesus, the Christ, and the Holy Spirit, I hereby renounce my position and my assignment with (name the person). I do this on behalf of myself and all of my group under my authority and I commit that we will never return or send others. This is our last assignment."**

Then tell the head demon: In the Name of the Lord Jesus Christ who arose on the third day, by the power of the Blood, the Cross and the Resurrection, and by His ascension whereby He now sits at the right hand of the Father God Almighty, I send you and all remaining demons to the feet of Jesus for judgment at the count of three: ONE, TWO, in Jesus' Name…THREE! OUT! Now call upon God's warring angels to use their swords and chop into little pieces any demons who are not gone. Then drop those pieces at the feet of Jesus.

At this point, I anoint the person with oil as a symbol of the Holy Spirit and by faith declare that the cross of the Lord Jesus is between them and all demonic activity. I put a seal on them by faith with the Blood of Jesus, declaring that the Blood is filling in the voids left by the demons and with the Holy Spirit according to the Word.

Lay on hands and speak healing as needed (see the chapter on physical healing).

Do a limb check for a short leg or arm, concerning their back/neck and/or squeezing of the brain stem or C1/C2. Command adjustment and for any pain to go.

This is also a great time to administer the Baptism of the Holy Spirit with speaking in tongues, if they have not previously received.

Speak God's blessings and peace over them.

If you think there are alters or protectors present in the person, I now proceed into the integration process as set out in the chapter, "True Multiple Personalities are not demons."

CHAPTER 10

USE GOD'S ANGELS

Hebrews 1:14 tells us, "Are not all angels ministering spirits sent to serve those who will inherit salvation?" This scripture is part of our salvation package. Why not use our angels? Angels are sent to us by God to serve us. Any Christian who is doing these works of Jesus (i.e., ministering to the broken-hearted, setting at liberty those who are bruised, preaching deliverance to the captives (Luke 4:18)) has much opportunity to utilize God's angels. Other Bible translations add that the ministering spirits are there to be "of service" to the heirs of salvation. We have experienced calling on angels to help us as we minister ... angels truly are there to be of service to Christians, if we activate them by faith.

In 1978, I was just learning about this ministry, as I was still learning to minister effectively, when three of us ministered to a young steelworker. He worked on high-rise buildings. He was very muscular, as you can imagine. We were ministering in the church office, when suddenly this young man violently lunged at Conn Davis (a retired Spirit-filled Methodist pastor) and knocked him over backwards out of the folding chair that he was sitting in ... he hit the carpet without being hurt. Immediately, the brother who was leading the deliverance said: "Violence, in Jesus' Name, be still." Suddenly, the young man could no longer move ... it seemed as though someone was holding him in place! We then proceeded with the ministry. How awesome! We were watching angels serving us right before our eyes.

I have often thought, "How blessed I am to have learned this early in my ministry." On occasion, I have had to use those same commands. We have learned to often add, "You are bound, in Jesus' Name." If the person has fallen out of his chair, then add, "You are bound to the floor." If the individual is still sitting in the chair, his fists are doubling up and he is starting to shake, then it is time to give the command, "You are bound to the chair." Every time I see evidence that the angels are there, holding their arms.

I ministered to a good-sized man in my office who was born in and attended high school in Germany. When we started ministry, I flushed up a demon who manifested and spoke right out of the person's mouth. As he identified himself, he said that it (the spirit) was a "German fighting spirit." It scooted the man backward in his chair as I came against it with my Bible in hand. He finally stopped as his chair came against my coffee table. But I could see his fists were doubled and his arms were shaking. — I took authority over this spirit ... I said, "You are bound to the chair." He got still and I continued with the ministry. The man told me later that the demon was telling him to throw me through the window. My office was on the 19th floor! However, because I knew my authority and because angels helped me, we successfully set him free from his oppression.

For many years, we did our Monday evening deliverance and healing sessions at my mortgage office. (We were always known as a full service company!) Normally, we would minister to around 10 or 12 people and usually had a volunteer minister available to minister individually to each person. After the teaching and preparation of those needing ministry, I would match the teams and the person wanting ministry.

One particular Monday evening, my wife, Carolyn, was helping me. As we ministered, we heard a ruckus taking place down the hall. I was deeply involved with the person I was ministering to, so I asked Carolyn to go check to see what was happening. Later, I found out that two men ministers were working with a man who was manifesting demonic activity, and had become violent. He had kicked a couple of files off the desk ... these two men were holding the man down on the floor! Carolyn came in, saw the situation, took authority, commanded the demons to be still ... that they were bound. Immediately, the man was quiet! The two men ministers, who were rather new in deliverance ministry, said, "Wow, how did you do that?"

It is wonderful that we Christians have power over all the enemy and nothing shall harm us! (Luke 10:19) Angels will back the Word and be of service to us as we speak the Word of God out loud.

We primarily teach basic deliverance techniques that are detailed in this book. We have seen that this process works very well with thousands of people. We include physical and emotional healing.

A few years ago, I ministered in a mass deliverance at a church in Enid, Oklahoma. We did some individual ministry thereafter. There were three of us: Craig Vickers of Enid, Oklahoma, John Sigmon of Norman, Oklahoma, who is one of our regular team leaders, and me.

A young man was sitting in a chair manifesting demonic activity when suddenly, he jumped up and ran toward the church door. We did not chase after him; instead, we called upon God's angels to bring him back and set him in the chair. The man returned, walking sideways, with something appearing to hold onto each arm, and he was plopped down in the chair!

This happened three times. Later, I thought, "Why didn't I ask the angels to hold him in his chair?" I guess I didn't realize that he would jump up again. It was an incredible demonstration of God's angels responding to our need.

A pastor called me about a 15-year-old young man who had been involved with alcohol and had been using drugs! The young man reached the point where he thought that he couldn't take it any more and decided to take his own life. He had a pistol in his mouth ... was ready to pull the trigger ... then, his pastor called (when the Holy Spirit prompted him). Supernatural intervention! The call stopped him from pulling the trigger. Then his pastor scheduled him for deliverance at our next Monday evening meeting of healing and deliverance. I made a commitment to minister to him that Monday night.

His parents brought him and sat on the back row. He looked rather spaced out and rebellious, pulling his baseball cap down over his face. A couple of times, he pulled his coat over his head. It was clear to me that he did not want to be there. You know, the people we seem to do the best with are those who are coming on their own, who are reaching out, saying: "Jesus, help me." So, I was thinking, "This is going to be a tough case." (I realized later the demons were at the surface and manifesting the whole time during the teaching and preparation.)

When I led the people through the pre-ministry, door-closing prayer, I observed that his mouth was not moving. I thought, "Great! This means heavy manifestations of demonic activity are likely to happen during ministry." As we sat down for ministry, he kept his baseball cap down over his face. I looked over the suspect list his parents had prepared for him and started into ministry.

He immediately went into a major manifestation of demonic activity. He thrashed out of the chair and slithered under the table. I asked God's angels to pull him out and put him back in the chair.

Something seemed to pull him out by the legs and sat him up in the chair! Praise God! I never touched him. The angels were serving me, again being of service to those heirs of salvation.

I continued confronting the demon that was up, that was manifesting, and suddenly, it was gone. After this took place, I was now talking with a typical 15-year-old, I was no longer talking to the demon. He was outgoing and jovial. He took off his baseball cap! Then I continued through the healing and deliverance process. By the end of the evening he went out free, full of joy and full of light.

I wondered why the session went so well, considering that he had not reached out himself. It finally occurred to me that it was because his parents were in agreement and the young man was still under their spiritual authority. This is something we always need to remember.

I recently ministered to a young woman, about 30 years old, at our regular Monday evening healing and deliverance meeting. I had a demon up, manifesting, when the demon, using her feet, pushed her back several chair lengths. I immediately asked the angels to bring her and the chair back. She and the chair were back in moments. At another point of time in the evening, the head demon had her hands clasped together so tightly her fingernails were cutting into the palms of her hands. I asked God's angels to pull the fingers loose … we watched as the fingers were pried up one finger at a time! God's angels were helping once again.

Make ministry easy on yourself … use God's angels.

CHAPTER 11

PHYSICAL HEALING

KEYS TO PHYSICAL HEALING

The Word tells me that our Jesus has already provided for our physical healing. It was part of our package from the cross. "When the evening was come, they bought unto Him many that were possessed with demons; and He cast out the spirits with His word, and healed ALL that were sick, that it might be fulfilled which was spoken by Isaiah, the prophet, saying, **He himself took our infirmities, and bore our sickness."** (Matthew 8:16-17)

"Who his own self bore our sins in His own body on the tree, that we, being dead to sins, should live unto righteousness; **by whose stripes ye were healed**." (1 Peter 2:24)

Under the anointing of the Holy Spirit and as you speak the Word, you **receive** healing. However, a certain number of people do not seem to keep their healing. In fact, healing may not be something you have experienced at all, even though you may have stood in many prayer lines. **What could be blocking your healing?**

Acts 10:38 tells us: "How God anointed Jesus of Nazareth with the Holy Spirit and with power, who went about doing good, and **healing all that were oppressed of the devil**; for God was with Him."

May I suggest a thought? Could there be a spirit of infirmity causing your illness? Jesus spoke of a spirit of infirmity... "And behold, there was a woman who had a spirit of infirmity eighteen years, and was bowed together and could in no way lift herself up. And when Jesus saw her, He called her to Him, and said unto her, 'Woman, thou are loosed from thine infirmity.'" (Luke:13:11-12)

If there is a spirit that is causing an illness or sickness, it may very well be there because it has a right to be there. Any evil spirit, including spirits of infirmity, can use the same doors to oppress your life. These doors were discussed in Chapter 4.

Unforgiveness is certainly the most major door that we see, even though you may have several open doors in your life that you are unaware of, such as curses, especially generational curses. Over and over I have seen healing blocked by not getting all the unforgiveness handled biblically. You choose to forgive and voice that forgiveness out loud and specifically; i.e., "I forgive you for offending me when you said..." Sometimes, bitterness needs to be released. Other times there are feelings of abandonment, rejection, anger or hurt that have been overlooked. It is most important to close all doors to the enemy of our soul so he/they don't have access to oppress us with infirmity. Consequently, it is imperative that people thoroughly break all ungodly soul ties.

If you want healing and you want to keep your healing, it is time to clean out all of the unforgiveness and bitterness. You need to speak it out to Jesus. Say the name of the person you are forgiving and declare that you forgive them for the specific offense. Then, declare that you bless them. (They may not deserve forgiveness. However, that is not the issue here. We forgive others and ourselves to set ourselves free.) If you can't remember the name, tell the Lord you forgive the person you are seeing in your mind. It may be someone who is not living today ... remember, unforgiveness is your problem and not the problem for the person you are forgiving. Forgive, get free, and keep your healing.

Another method that can be helpful is to ask Jesus to take you back to the root of the infirmity or sickness. This is probably a memory in the past. He might take you back to a specific event when you were offended or abused as a child, or to some other event in your past that needs to be addressed with forgiveness and inner healing. Once you forgive, be sure to ask Jesus to reveal Himself to you in that situation, to speak truth to you, to love you, to comfort you, and show that He cares for you.

Stress and anxiety may be a root cause of your sickness. Ask Jesus to take you back to those early roots. Ask Him to speak truth into those memories. (See the inner healing Chapter 8.) Spirits of stress and anxiety may need to be renounced and cast out before healing can be received. Again, be sure you have broken all possible generational curses and satanic assignments.

Remember to apply the seven keys for staying free. They apply to keeping your healing as well. (Chapter 14)

HEALING OF BACKS AND NECKS

In 1978, I was introduced to the healing of backs. The little Full Gospel church that I joined after receiving the Baptism of the Holy Spirit ministered the healing of backs. As a result, I have seen hundreds and probably thousands of backs healed by using a simple method of prayer.

A retired, Spirit-filled, Methodist preacher, Pastor Con Davis, first showed me how God wanted to demonstrate His power. He showed me how to be a doer of the Word and **speak in Jesus' Name ... command, in Jesus' Name, "adjust and be healed. Pain, go!"** (Mark 16:17 & John 14:12)

If someone is complaining about pain in their back or neck, ask them sit down in a straightback chair, sit as balanced as they can; then, with their permission, hold up their feet side by side so that you can see the <u>heels</u> of their shoes. Many times you will see one leg is shorter than the other. You may see one leg is shorter by a half to three-quarters of an inch, sometimes more. I have seen as much as three inches difference in the length of their legs. (If the problem is the upper back or neck, there may be a short arm) Usually all I need to say is the simple command, **"In Jesus' Name, adjust, pain go."**

If, after 20-30 seconds, there is no change, ask them the question, "Who do you need to forgive?" (They may need to forgive someone else or themselves.) If there is no remaining unforgiveness and you do not see any change, break curses, demonic assignments and rebuke any spirits of infirmity, especially of the back/neck. "I break every curse spoken against _____ (name of person) and break all generational curses, in Jesus' Name ... I break all demonic assignments, in Jesus' Name ... I command all spirits of infirmity to go." **COMMAND** them to go to the feet of Jesus. Also, **COMMAND** permanent neurotransmitter balance, in Jesus' Name.

Once you have seen adjustment in their lower vertebrae and legs, evidenced by seeing the legs grow out and become even, it is time to adjust the hips, the arms and the neck. Ask them to place their hands on their pelvic bones ... then, **COMMAND** the pelvic bones to adjust and the tailbone to adjust. **COMMAND** pain to go, the electrical and magnetic systems to be balanced. Once that is accomplished, ask them to stand with their feet approximately six inches apart, even at the toes, lift their arms in front of you with the fingers one inch apart, and **COMMAND "In Jesus' Name, adjust, pain go."** Then, move to the neck. Place the tips of your fingers in the middle of the back of the neck. Wrap your hands around with your palms resting on the cheeks. **COMMAND** adjustment, alignment, healing and release any pressure to the brain stem, spine, neck, C1, C2, the muscles, tendons, ligaments, and nerves. **COMMAND "In Jesus' Name, adjust, pain go." Rebuke pain again. COMMAND this a number of times.** Add any other commands that the Holy Spirit might show you while you are commanding adjustment to their spine ... speaking specifically to the person's specific problem. Remember, this is normal Christianity...not a special gift.

If it still does not adjust, go back over unforgiveness again. Often they need to get more **specific** regarding forgiving. Name a particular individual, themselves or God, forgive, and the short limb will shoot out – this shows the adjustment has taken place. **Sometimes other healing takes place in their body as you pray this way. (Probably because the brain stem or C1/**

C2 is freed up.) I ask them to stand up and do something they couldn't do before, to check for pain. The pain will be gone. If not, go back through a third time, especially looking for more specific unforgiveness, hurt, bitterness, resentment, offense, rejection, or anger that needs to be released, etc. I also put my hand or the Bible on the spot, rebuking the pain and commanding permanent healing.

Several years ago, my son in-law was over at our house for Thanksgiving. He mentioned his back was hurting. We went through this process. But in the rush, I forgot to ask if he had any unforgiveness toward himself. Nevertheless, his short leg came out, the pain was gone and he enjoyed the turkey. However, the next day he called me saying "The pain is back." This time I thought to ask him if he needed to forgive himself. He said, "Well, that might be a problem." I said, "Ken...do it!" As he forgave himself while we were speaking on the phone, his pain left and has been gone for several years now! He still talks about his healing. **God has made his point: Unforgiveness will block deliverance and healing.**

ADDITIONAL INSIGHTS INTO PHYSICAL HEALING

Be sure that you have completed the door-closing prayer, broken all ungodly soul ties that you were aware of, experienced inner healing of emotional wounds, and commanded the possible list of evil spirits to go to the feet of Jesus during deliverance thoroughly (**especially spirits of unforgiveness, self-bitterness, anger, bitterness, fear, trauma, death, destruction, infirmity, stress, worry, depression, disappointment**).

If healing has not taken place when you have accomplished these tasks, then it is time to use the biblical mandate of laying-on-of-hands (even on yourself) and pray the following in the name of Jesus and by the resurrection power of the Holy Spirit. **Remember, as a born again Christian, you have the power to command.** (Luke 10:17-19, Mark 11:23-24)

1. Command your heart rate variability to be balanced.
2. Command your nervous system to be balanced.
3. Command any cells that are shut down to open.
4. Command any ungodly cellular memory to be terminated, in Jesus' Name.
5. Command "My cells are Jesus-energized and come into the balanced growth mode, now, in Jesus' Name."
6. Command your Ph levels to be godly adjusted and that your cells are oxygenated in Jesus' Name and by the power of the Holy Spirit.
7. Command the electrical, chemical and magnetic frequencies along with the DNA of each of your cells to be godly balanced by the power of the Holy Spirit.

8. Command your immune system to be 100% efficient.
9. Command your good cells to devour any bad cells (such as cancer cells, etc.) Open your spiritual eyes to see your good cells doing this job like a little Pac-man on dots. Focus on this for a while, until you see in your spiritual mind all bad cells eaten up and destroyed. Curse the root of all bad cells in Jesus' Name.
10. Speak directly to your situation, command your healing, and declare that you are healed. **See yourself** and **feel yourself (in your spirit man)** totally healed. (Mark 11:23-24)
11. Praise and thank the Lord for His blessings in your life.

I suggest that you do the above steps a number of times on a daily basis until your healing is realized.

CHAPTER 12

MINISTERING TO CHILDREN

Satan has so many ways to torment our children today. Children have always been targets … just as they were in the days of the New Testament.

"For a certain woman, whose young daughter had an unclean spirit, heard of Him, and came and fell at His feet." (Mark 7:25)

Another scripture, Mark 9:17-21, Jesus cast a dumb spirit out of a young man. His father said it had come in him "as a child."

I have seen a rash of children being tormented because of our modern-day electronic world and games. It is wonderful that these medias are being used to promote the Gospel. However, Satan has not lost any time in using them for his benefit.

Innocent as the cartoons may seem, many are used to plant demonic oppression in our children. Even when parents are selective with their children, the enemy is getting hits in on them. The cartoons are a convenient babysitting tool; however, parents have the responsibility to protect their children.

Scary movies can be used by the enemy of our souls to open another door to the demonic realm. One day, when I was ministering, a demon told me it had come into this child of God through Halloween. Another young lady could not stay free from fear until she took a rock group poster down from her bedroom wall.

A strong, Spirit-filled woman was bothered with a spirit of fear. This spirit of fear was blocking her from taking on volunteer responsibilities in her church. After two sessions of deliverance, I was able to get the head demon up and talking to me. This head demon disclosed that fear came in when she was a youngster by reading a book called "Grimm's Fairy Tales." When she got rid of the book of fairy tales, she was set free.

A baby was about to die from not eating until a devil-like doll that was in the crib was taken away, unknowingly put there by a grandmother. Their pediatrician was the one who found the devil doll because she was Spirit-filled and discerned the doll was evil. After getting rid of the doll the baby was set free.

The Bible tells us to give no place to the devil. (Ephesians 4:27) What is in your home that might be giving rights to the enemy to torment you and your children? Do you have occult materials in your home? What about objects that represent other religions or even demons? Does everything in your home glorify God? Do you have books, movies or games that are doorways into the evil supernatural?

I ministered to one of my granddaughters when she was five and was being tormented by a spirit of fear that had initially come in through cartoons. As we ministered to her, she got set free. Later, the fear spirit to came back on her, oppressing her as the result of visiting the house of a little girlfriend whose older brother was into Pokemon. The girls also watched a Harry Potter movie. When we ministered to my granddaughter the second time, she actually vomited the spirit up.

Parents, be careful what activities you allow when your children spend the night at a friend's house. Be careful about the activities that you allow in your own home. It may look cute, but it may be deadly for your children.

Pokemon cartoons, as well as playing with the Pokeman cards, etc., along with other similar games are resulting in demonized kids. I remember interviewing a father on my radio show about what happened to their 11-year-old son. Their son had a speech disorder that had gotten so severe the local doctors sent them to the Mayo Clinic in Minnesota for a week of tests ... with no results. The frustrated parents brought their son to Deliverance Ministries. In one ministry session, these parents saw a breakthrough for their son. The final deliverance came after they burned the cards he had been playing with.

Another recent case ... a 12-year-old boy had become extremely rebellious, controlling, destructive, and was having fits of violence and rage about eight months before ministry. A spirit of hate manifested and spoke out of him. He had been into Pokemon as well as violent games. We got him set free. But, he went to a friend's house, got involved again with Pokeman, and the spirits came back. After another deliverance session, he experienced victory!

WE CHRISTIANS ARE IN A SPIRITUAL WAR FOR OUR CHILDREN!

We have seen situations where the parents have received deliverance and the minor children are automatically set free. There were times when the children were not even present during the ministry sessions! In other cases, children have needed more direct ministry, either by the parents or by a deliverance minister, with at least one parent present. Ministry can be very effective with the child sleeping. The same type of spirits as shown in the problem or suspect list can bother children, as well as all types of infirmity spirits, generational or otherwise. The parents or guardian can usually fill out the list of problems for the child and add a few that are suspicious.

Please consider that there may be a "spirit guide or familiar spirit" posing as a little "elf" friend to your child. It may be the parent has seen the child talking with something that cannot be seen. It may be an invisible playmate that seems to be an imaginary friend. Usually the child will think it is a friend. However, we know that the spirit is there to steal, kill, and destroy the child at some point. During the period of time that the parents have the spiritual authority over their children as born again Christians, it is important to renounce and to rebuke it. It would be ideal for the child to do it with them. Finding out the name of the spirit and breaking off an ungodly soul tie with the child would be even better.

Often we do not see any manifestations at all with children, and it is not unusual that they may not see any results for two or three weeks.

Even though we have done it many different ways, we have found that it is best for the parents to go through ministry first. At that time, parents can address generational curses, break them, and break off any curses coming from their parents as well. Then, after a couple of weeks, see how the children are doing.

It is always good to explain to the child how there are bad (evil) spirits around that bother people, even children. These bad spirits can cause children to do things they do not want to do. In Jesus' Name, we all have **ALL** power over these bad spirits. So, when you start telling these bad spirits to go, you are not speaking to the children, but to the bad spirits. You can make a game out of it telling them it is fun to get rid of the bad spirits by using your Jesus gun. Show them how to use their index finger and thumb as their gun and say, "In Jesus' Name, go."

A basic checklist:

1. Parent(s) or the person who is in authority pray the door closing over the children. If any of the children want to repeat the door closing, that is better. Quote Luke 10:19.
2. Break ungodly soul ties and ask Jesus to speak truth to the children about those relationships.
3. Ask Jesus to bring truth and emotional healing to them concerning their traumas.
4. Command possible demons on the problem or suspect list to go to the feet of Jesus for judgment as it applies to the child.
5. Command any remaining evil spirits to go.
6. Declare that they are sealed by the Blood of Jesus, the anointing of the Holy Spirit and the peace of God that passes all understanding, keeping their hearts and minds in Christ Jesus.
7. Minister physical healing.

Usually, deliverance is easier with children than with adults. I have seen effective ministry take place by even skipping steps 2 and 3. However, it is important to be thorough.

I learned from Dr. Charles Kraft, of Fuller Seminary in California, that even during pregnancy, the parents or a parent should dedicate the child to Jesus, while still in the womb. During this dedication prayer, break off all curses, and rebuke any associated evil spirits, commanding them to go to the feet of Jesus. It is best to do this as early in the pregnancy as possible. We have found that the end result is that these babies seem to behave marvelously in all respects after they are born. The light of Jesus, the blood of Jesus, and the anointing of the Holy Spirit make more of a difference in a child's life when all possible assignments of the dark side are broken before birth.

CHAPTER 13

STEPS TO STAY FREE AND FULL OF LIFE

HOW TO STAY FREE AND HEALED (PART I)

Jesus used deliverance ministry to bring freedom to those oppressed by the devil. After being set free, pay careful attention to the following points that will allow you to continue to live in freedom and maintain healing:

• Read the Word out loud each day.	II Timothy 3:16-17
• Pray (talk to God conversationally) everyday.	Ephesians 6:18
• Have Christian fellowship.	Matthew 18:19-20
• Keep the doors closed.	Galatians 5:16-26
• Resist the devil, speaking the Word.	James 4:7
• Strengthen your spirit man by confessing or declaring daily the positives, the Word of God and declaring the promises of God.	Mark 11:22-25; Eph. 1:3-23; 3:16
• Make godly choices.	Deuteronomy 30:19

Then you will know the truth, and the truth will set you free. (John 8.32)

Let's discuss these.

1. READ THE WORD OUT LOUD EVERY DAY

Most of us seldom miss three meals a day... we are very good at feeding our physical person, but what about our spirit person? Often our spirit man/woman is starved. We need to feed ourselves the Word. We need to read at least a few scriptures each day, hopefully more.

"All Scripture is given by inspiration of God, and is profitable for doctrine, for reproof, for correction, for instruction in righteousness, That the man of God may be perfect, thoroughly furnished unto all good works." (II Timothy 3:16-17)

Read and learn the Word, then speak it out loud. Declare the Word of God; the Word will perform itself as a Christian speaks it; it will not return void. "So shall My word be that goes forth from My mouth; it shall not return to Me void. But it shall accomplish what I please, And it shall prosper in the thing for which I sent it. (Isaiah 55:11)

When Jesus was tempted by the devil or man, He always responded, "It is written....." Jesus' weapon against the devil was the Word of God. **We need to do the same. Deliverance and healing come as Christians quote the Word.**

"And Jesus answered him, saying, 'It is written, man shall not live by bread alone, but by every word of God.'" (Luke 4:4)

"And Jesus answered and said unto him, 'Get thee behind Me, Satan; for it is written, Thou shalt worship the Lord thy God, and Him only shalt thou serve.'" (Luke 4:8)

Quoting scriptures on deliverance and healing are especially important after ministry.

We read in Luke 10:19 that in His Name, we have power and authority over ALL the enemy (demonic forces) and the promise that nothing will hurt us. In Mark 16:17, we as believers are commissioned (even commanded) to cast out evil spirits and to lay hands on the sick and they will be healed.

Following is an excellent list of scriptures telling us who we are in Christ, as taught in the Word. Pick out the ones that are especially meaningful to you, adding to the list additional scriptures that are meaningful to you; then, quote or declare them often.

I AM (say out loud)

1. A child of God (Romans 8:16)
2. Redeemed from the hand of the enemy (Psalm 107:2)
3. Forgiven (Colossians 1:13-14)
4. Saved by Grace through Faith (Ephesians 2:8)
5. Righteous and holy (Ephesians 4:24)

6. Justified (just as if I never sinned) (Romans 5:1)
7. Sanctified (1 Corinthians 6:11)
8. A New Creature (2 Corinthians 5:17)
9. Partaker of His Divine Nature (2 Peter 1:4)
10. Redeemed from the curse of the Law (Galatians 3:13)
11. Delivered from the powers of darkness (Colossians 1:13)
12. Led by the Spirit of God (Romans 8:14)
13. A Son of God (Romans 8:14)
14. Hidden with Christ in God (Colossians 3:3)
15. The salt of the earth (Matthew 5:13)
16. The light of the world (Matthew 5:14)
17. Part of the true vine (John 15:1-2)
18. Chosen by God, holy and dearly loved by God (Colossians 3:12)
19. Kept in safety wherever I go (Psalm 91:11)
20. Getting all my needs met by my Lord Jesus Christ (Philippians 4:19)
21. Casting all my cares on My Lord Jesus (1 Peter 5:7)
22. Strong in the Lord and in the power of His might (Ephesians 6:10)
23. Doing all things through Christ who strengthens me (Philippians 4:13)
24. An heir of God and a joint heir with my Lord Jesus Christ (Romans 8:17)
25. Observing and doing the Lord's commandments (Deuteronomy 28:12)
26. Blessed coming in and blessed going out (Deuteronomy 28:6)
27. Blessed [INDWELT BY GOD AND HIS KINGDOM] (Deuteronomy 28:6)
28. Blessed with the blessing of Abraham. (Galatians 3:13-15)
29. An inheritor of eternal life (1 John 5:11-12)
30. Blessed with all spiritual blessings (Ephesians 1:3)
31. Healed by His stripes (1 Peter 2:24)
32. Exercising my authority over the enemy (Luke 10:19)
33. Above only and not beneath (Deuteronomy 28:13)
34. More than a conqueror (Romans 8:37)
35. Establishing God's Word here on earth (Matthew 16:19)
36. An overcomer by the Blood of the Lamb and the word of my testimony (Rev. 12:11)
37. Submitting to God and resisting the devil (James 4:7)
38. Daily overcoming the devil (1 John 4:4)
39. Not moved by what I see (2 Corinthians 4:18)
40. Walking by faith and not by sight (2 Corinthians 10:4-5
41. Casting down vain imaginations (2 Corinthians 10:4-5)
42. Bringing every thought into captivity in Christ Jesus (2 Corinthians 10:5)
43. Being transformed by the renewing of my mind (Romans 12:1-2)
44. A laborer (partner-NLT) together with God (1 Corinthians 3:9)

45. The righteousness of God in Christ Jesus (2 Corinthians 5:21)
46. An imitator or follower of Jesus Christ (Ephesians 5:1)

HOW TO STAY FREE AND HEALED (PART II)

2. PRAY EVERY DAY

Our Jesus wants us to pray to Him and talk with Him. To express our needs. "Let us, therefore, come boldly before the throne of grace, that we may obtain mercy, and find grace to help in time of need. (Hebrews 4:16)

Prayer is conversation with the Lord. Talk with Him just as you would talk to any other friend. It doesn't make any difference whether you're at home, or in the office or in the car. It doesn't make any difference whether you bow your head, or close your eyes, or kneel. Prayer is not a position of the body, but an attitude of the heart.

"Whatsoever ye ask in My Name, that will I do, that the Father may be glorified in the Son." And if ye shall ask anything in My Name, I will do it." (John 14:13-14)

And just as in any other conversation, there is a time to talk, and a time to listen. Tell Him your needs...and listen to His answers. Ask Him to put His arms around you and to bring His truth to you, to point out any lies that you are hearing and accepting from the enemy.

Paul tells us in Romans 8:26-27 that the prayer language is especially helpful when we have a need, but don't know what it is or how to express it to God, or for what solution we should ask: "Likewise, the Spirit also helpeth our infirmities; for we know not what we should pray for, as we ought; but the Spirit, Himself, maketh intercession for us with groanings which cannot be uttered. And He that searcheth the hearts, knoweth what is the mind of the Spirit, because He maketh intercession for the saints according to the will of God."

Paul also said in 1 Corinthians 14:14-15, "For if I pray in an unknown tongue, my spirit prayeth, but my understanding is unfruitful. What is it then? I will pray with the understanding also; I will sing with the spirit and I will sing with the understanding also."

Jude 20, I think, is very clear about our need to pray in the spirit, "But you, beloved, build yourselves up on your most holy faith; praying in the Holy Spirit."

I think it is also excellent to speak the protective Blood of Jesus (Revelation 12:11) over yourself, your family, your home, your activities, your ministries, your work, your health, your possessions, and even your pets. Break curses and spells that may have been spoken over all these, as well. If you know or feel that a certain person has spoken curses or spells over you, name them as the originator. Sometimes people speak curses without realizing the power of the tongue. Be sure to forgive those people and bless them. "Death and life are in the power of the tongue, and they that love it shall eat the fruit thereof." (Proverbs 18:21)

3. KEEP CHRISTIAN FELLOWSHIP

I have been to Alaska several times and I have seen the herds of caribou moving in the Alaskan wilds. Even if you have not been to Alaska, you are probably familiar with caribou from watching nature movies. As long as a herd of caribou stays together, there is protection from the wolf packs that stalk them, but if a caribou drifts away from the herd, the wolves are always waiting and will move right in. He's alone, and he doesn't have the protection of the herd.

That's the way it is with us as well. As long as we keep Christian fellowship, as long as we're in a group of believers, the devil is not as likely to attack. Especially if we are in agreement. There is a danger of being a loaner without the power of agreement. When you resist in the name of Jesus, you win! Ask someone else to join with you; there is power in agreement.

"Again I say unto you, that if two of you shall agree on earth as touching anything that they shall ask, it shall be done for them of My Father, which is in heaven. For where two or three are gathered together in My Name, there am I in the midst of them." (Matthew 18:19-20)

"And five of you shall chase a hundred and a hundred of you shall put ten thousand to flight, and your enemies shall fall before you by the sword." (Leviticus 26:8)

We've found that there is no substitute for the blessings of strength and help that fellowshipping with other Christians gives us. And of course I recommend a church that is teaching <u>ALL</u> the gospel. You experience the anointing of the Holy Spirit in a profound way through corporate worship.

4. KEEP THE DOORS CLOSED TO SATAN

The doors we went over in Chapter 5 are entries that we have seen demons often use, and some of these doors you probably noticed, are really easy to open. You can get free in a ministry session, and open a door next week. Someone may do you wrong, so what are you going to do? Follow the flesh with bitterness and wanting revenge, or do what the Bible says? Remember, Jesus said if you don't forgive, you will be turned to the tormentors. It's not that hard once you have some understanding of how demons operate and who you are in Jesus. It's your option to "not give place to the devil." (Ephesians 4:27)

5. RESIST THE DEVIL

It is possible an evil spirit might try to come back following deliverance, even if you have not opened a door. If that should happen, you need to remember the Word. How much power and authority do you have? One hundred percent, if you will use it! (Luke 10:19) Too many Christians leave their guns in their holsters.

Shirley Clark had come for ministry because she had been tormented for most of her life with a fear of public speaking. Her company had started sending her out to do seminars. She was miserable and would sometimes even throw up before. She finally came for ministry. I happened to work with her. Her husband was sitting there as I got hold of this spirit. It was hurting her in the chest, finally moving up into her throat, choking her, as she reported later. It finally departed, with great relief, and she now enjoyed doing the seminars....for six months! Shirley was in Chicago, in her hotel room before going down for the seminar, and this fear spirit started hanging around. Shirley panicked, finally getting down on her knees, crying out to the Lord, "Lord, help me, I can't handle this...do something." Well, the Lord spoke to her saying, "Shirley, get off of you knees, stand up and tell that spirit of fear to go, in My Name!" She stood up, told it to go in His Name, and it did! Shirley resisted the spirit **herself, in His Name**. She went ahead and did the seminar ... and with great joy! She has been free for many years now.

What does the word say? "Submit yourself to God, then **resist** the devil and he will flee." (James 4:7)

"Be sober, be vigilant, because your adversary, the devil, like a roaring lion walketh about, seeking whom he may devour; whom **resist** steadfast in the faith, knowing that the same afflictions are accomplished in your brethren that are in the world. (1 Peter 5:8-9)

And of course, we resist with **ALL** power and **ALL** authority in His Name. (Luke 10:19) Our power in God is UNLIMINTED. Our weapons are not carnal (of this world). Our weapons are spiritual and absolute – mighty through God to the pulling down of strongholds.

"For the weapons of our warfare are not carnal, but mighty through God to the pulling down of strongholds, casting down imaginations, and every high thing that exalteth itself against the knowledge of God, and bringing into captivity every thought to the obedience of Christ." (II Corinthians 10:4)

Remember, our weapons in Jesus are stronger than Satan's weapons... **if you will use them!**

6. CONFESS GOD'S POSITIVES

After I got into the Word in 1978, I started realizing some things. I had not understood that by speaking certain negatives, those negatives can be a curse in the spirit world, thereby giving demonic forces the right to torment. I had to start watching my tongue and how I used it.

The Bible says:" Death and life are in the power of the tongue, and they that love it shall eat the fruit thereof." (Proverbs 18:21)

If we speak negatives about someone or ourselves, that's what tends to happen. It is a better deal to speak God's positives and then receive God's positives.

"For verily I say unto you, That whosoever shall say unto this mountain, be thou removed, and be thou cast into the sea; and shall not doubt in his heart, but shall believe that those things which he saith shall come to pass; he **shall have whatsoever he saith**. Therefore I say unto you, what things soever ye desire, when ye pray, believe ye receive them and ye shall have them." (Mark 11:23-24)

So, if we get what we say, let's **speak the positives of the Word out loud,** knowing the Word will perform itself as a Christian speaks it out loud. The Word will not return void, accomplishing that for which it is sent. Find scriptures that represent what you need in your life and speak them out. (Isaiah 55:1)

"Then said the Lord unto me, thou hast well seen; **for I will hasten my word to perform it**." (Jeremiah 1:12)

7. MAKE GODLY CHOICES

You and I will have a "fork" in the road before us the rest of our lives. One road is the ungodly road and the other is the godly road. Since God made us in His image (Genesis 1:26), we can <u>choose</u> anything we wish. We are beings of self-will. My counsel to you: choose God's road. You can't just sit there, you have to choose one or the other.

"I call heaven and earth to record this day against you, that I have set before you life and death, blessing and cursing: therefore **choose** life, that both thou and thy seed may live." (Deuteronomy 30:19)

You will have constant choices to make. There will be "forks" in the road on giving, such as giving your money, your time, your energy, ministering to the hurting people, doing whatever your ministry is. The blessings of doing these will come around the circle back to you. Likewise, giving to the storehouse that is doing the works of Jesus, to the poor, those in need as the Lord leads. There are many ways to give. You can expect God's blessings as you do.

"Give, and it shall be given unto you, good measure, pressed down, and shaken together, and running over, shall men give into your bosom. For with the same measure that ye mete withal it shall be measured to you again." (Luke 6:38)

DELIVERANCE AND HEALING IN HOLY COMMUNION

A few years ago, I was listening to Evangelist Sid Roth on his radio show as he interviewed Dr. John Miller from Florida. Dr. Miller was talking about how he had studied for 25 years the benefits of taking Holy Communion often, including daily in your home, and sometimes more than once a day. He stated how he has seen exciting miracles take place as a result. He said, "If we would focus on the bread as the actual body of the sacrificial lamb (Jesus), and the wine or symbolic wine as the actual blood of the sacrificial lamb (Jesus), the blessings of the new covenant would manifest."

I take communion often now and have made it a part of our Monday evening ministry session with the teams before ministry.

Here is how I usually take Holy Communion:

Holding the bread and the wine (or symbolic wine). "Jesus, we come together now to honor You, to worship You. We thank You for being the sacrificial lamb for all of mankind who will accept You for who You are and what You did for us. Father, we ask that You sanctify this bread as the body of the Sacrificial Lamb, Jesus.

"Jesus, as you said at the last supper, take of the bread and eat, that this is Your body broken for us, we do this in remembrance of You. Father, we ask that You sanctify this bread as the body of the Lamb, Jesus. As we take the bread, we eat it (begin to chew on the bread) on behalf of ourselves, our families, and the people who come for ministry. We acknowledge that every need in our lives has been met by what You did for us at the cross. As we eat of the body of the Lamb, we declare that every spiritual attack set up against us is now permanently cancelled, that we are healed (as you eat of the Sacrificial Lamb, the bread, see your particular need healed), physically healed, mentally healed, emotionally healed, and that Jesus became poor that we may prosper (thereby healing us financially). Glory to the Lamb, Jesus.

"Jesus, You also said to take of the wine (or symbolic wine) and drink, that this is Your blood shed for us. Father, we ask that You sanctify this wine as the blood of the Lamb, Jesus. As we drink now, we declare this as a seal of the blessings of the new covenant, spiritually, physically, mentally, emotionally, financially. We thank You, Lord, that there is redemption in this blood, deliverance, and healing in the blood for spiritual warfare, long, healthy, productive life in the blood, abundance in the blood and power in the blood. Glory to the Lamb, Jesus."

I highly recommend that you take Holy Communion often, especially after you have received ministry, in fact, the rest of your life. **There is life in the blood!**

CHAPTER 14

THE POWER OF GOD

WHY THE BAPTISM OF THE HOLY SPIRIT?

John 3:34:	If there are measures of the Holy Spirit. Would we not want a full measure?
Acts 8:14-17:	Apostles at Jerusalem ... They went about administering the Holy Spirit by the laying on of hands because the believers were only baptized in the Name of the Lord Jesus.
Acts 10:44-47:	They spoke with tongues ... We can see that speaking with tongues is associated with having the fullness of the Holy Spirit. (Example of the Holy Spirit baptism first, then water.)
Acts 19:1-7:	Example of water baptism first, then baptism in the Holy Spirit by speaking in tongues.
Mark 16:17:	Jesus said to speak in new tongues. (It is interesting to note that in all four gospels, Jesus never baptized with water ... only the Holy Spirit. However, water baptism is also needed, according to the scriptures.)
1 Corinthians 14:18:	Paul spoke in tongues more than anyone.

IF JESUS TOLD BELIEVERS TO SPEAK IN TONGUES, AND PAUL SAID HE DID, IT MUST BE IMPORTANT FOR US. WHY? THIS IS THE OUTWARD EVIDENCE OF THE BAPTISM OF THE HOLY SPIRIT, WHICH IS FOR POWER AND:

1 Corinthians 14:2:	**You are speaking to God, not to man.**
1 Corinthians 14:4:	**You build up yourself, you edify yourself.**

Luke 11:9-13: If you have <u>asked</u> for the Holy Spirit, I believe <u>He has come.</u> This means you <u>get</u> to speak with tongues ... it's just that you may not have done it yet!

AGAIN, WHY DO YOU WANT TO SPEAK IN TONGUES? SO THE ANOINTING WILL RISE TO A HIGH MEASURE AND:

- ✞ For self-edification.
- ✞ So you don't overlook something that needs to be prayed to God.
- ✞ For the Gifts of the Holy Spirit to manifest.
- ✞ For the Power of the Holy Spirit to rise to a high measure.

To receive, you simply ask Jesus to baptize you in the Holy Spirit. Acts 2:4: They spoke ... How does anyone speak? You use your mouth, your vocal cords, your tongue. Then the Holy Spirit gives you the utterance, the sounds, the words that you will not understand. This is all your option ... to start and stop your tongue as you will. **SEE THE LIST OF BENEFITS THE HOLY SPIRIT BRINGS TO YOU LISTED BELOW:**

SOME OF WHAT THE HOLY SPIRIT BRINGS US AND DOES FOR US

Power to witness	Acts 1:8, Acts 10:38
Comforts	John 14:16, John 14:26
Leads us into all truth	John 14:17, John 15:26, John 16:13
Brings us remembrance	John 14:26
Convicts us of sin	John 16:8
Shows us the future	John 16:13
Brings us wisdom	Acts 6:3
Gives us joy	Acts 13:52, Romans 14:17
Leads us	Acts 13:4, Acts 20:28
Gives us peace	Romans 14:17

Sanctifies us	Romans 15:16
Teaches us	1 Corinthians 2:13
Gives us kindness	2 Corinthians 6:6
Gives us miracles and gifts	Hebrews 2:4
Speaks to us	Hebrews 3:7
Moves us	2 Peter 1:21
Builds us up	Jude 20
Anoints us	1 John 2:27
Speaks through us	Mark 13:11
Teaches us what to say	Luke 12:12
Teaches us all things	John 14:26

ADMINISTERING THE BAPTISM OF THE HOLY SPIRIT WITH SPEAKING IN OTHER TONGUES

At the end of a ministry session, I usually ask people if they have received the Baptism of the Holy Spirit with speaking in other tongues. I learned to always ask, "with the speaking in other tongues?" If they say no, then I ask, "Would you like to?" If the they are not sure, then I usually give them my testimony about what it did for me and how I received a boldness and power that led to the ministry that I do today (Acts 1:8).

I like to ask people if they have ever asked Jesus to baptize them in the Holy Spirit (Luke 11:9-18). If they say yes, I tell them that I believe that they received at that time, now they get to speak with other tongues if they will just open their mouth and do it.

Sometimes, they will say they believe they received the Holy Spirit when they were born again. I always agree with this, because it is true that they were drawn to salvation and received a measure of the Holy Spirit when they were saved. The Bible says in John 3:34, "Jesus received the Holy Spirit without measure." This implies that there are measures of the Holy Spirit.

Certainly the Baptism of the Holy Spirit with speaking in other tongues is evidence of a full measure.

Sometimes, people will say they are not sure they want or need to speak in other tongues. I like to open the Bible and show them that Jesus said, "believers shall speak in other tongues" (Mark 16:17), and Paul said he spoke "in other tongues more than anyone" (1 Corinthians 14:18). **Who has a higher authority to say we should not?**

Paul clarified why we want to have our tongues or prayer language.

Paul said, "he that speaketh in an unknown tongue speaketh not unto men but unto God" (1 Corinthians 14:2). In other words, we are praying to God what needs to be prayed at that time ... since we don't always know what to pray or how to pray. Speaking in tongues mysteries to God Himself is an excellent advantage in our Christian walk.

Paul also said, "He that speaketh in an unknown tongue edifieth himself" (1 Cor. 14:4). That is, he is building himself up, like charging a battery. Who does not need this? It's a tough world here.

It is interesting to note that Jesus is the one who would baptize with the Holy Spirit, as prophesied in all four of the Gospels.

You will hear people say they have asked Jesus to baptize them in the Holy Spirit, but have never been able to receive their prayer language. I think some people are waiting for a bolt of lightening or for the Holy Spirit to take them over and make them speak. I like to point out Acts 2:4, where we read "**they** (There were 120 assembled there) **were all filled with the Holy Ghost, and began to speak with other tongues, as the Spirit gave them utterance.**"

You can see that the 120 spoke in other tongues; i.e., other languages. How does anyone speak? By opening their mouth and using their vocal cords. You initiate with some sounds or mumblings. If you keep your mouth closed, nothing will come out. So here is our part: We use our physical vocal cords; then, the Holy Spirit gives the supernatural utterance, the words of our prayer language.

It is important to understand again that we are always in control, that we can start and stop our prayer language or tongues any time we wish. I sometimes show the person at this point by speaking in tongues for 15 or 20 seconds. I point out that I was in total control to start and stop, and that I did not understand what I just said. It was the Holy Spirit giving the utterance, the words to speak coming up from my inner man or heart.

When people say they are ready, I ask them to repeat after me:

"Jesus, thank You for the ministry you have given me. If You have more for me, then I am ready. I know I need the power, it's a tough world here. So Jesus, I ask You to baptize me in the Holy Spirit. Holy Spirit, by faith I receive You, the fullness of You, and my prayer language." I then say to the person, "Now raise your hands up to Jesus."

I lay my hand on their head saying, "Receive ye the Holy Spirit." I now commence speaking in tongues. One of three things happens at this point:

- ✓ They begin speaking immediately as a flowing language comes right out.
- ✓ The individual receives a few mumblings (as a start).
- ✓ Nothing comes out at this time. In the next day or two they speak as they are relaxed in private and their eyes are on Jesus.

I have seen it help some people to get started by saying, "Just speak out some sounds or vowels to get started," … and I will lead them in this, finally rolling on into my own prayer language.

If they were able to speak some, then I like to suggest we go one more time so they can see they can start their tongues any time they wish.

Then, I usually give them the Baptism of the Holy Spirit handout (the first two pages of this chapter), or you can show them the scriptures in the first part of this chapter so they can look up some of the scriptures and read what the fullness of Holy Spirit brings to us.

CHAPTER 15

ALL CHRISTIANS ARE CALLED TO CAST OUT DEMONS

NOW IT'S YOUR TURN TO MINISTER

A certain number of Christians think that they need a special gift to pray for people to get delivered, healed, etc. While there are some people who do have a special gift in these areas and a special anointing, I want to point something out…**the Word will perform itself as Christians speak it!**

The Word (Jesus) says that **believers** shall cast out devils and lay hands on the sick and they will recover (Mark 16:17). And I love this one: "He sent his word and healed them and delivered them from their destructions" (Psalm 107:20). And of course, the Word was made flesh … Jesus (John 1:14).

I have seen this from time to time after a Monday evening ministry session where our teams have ministered to around 10-15 people one-on-one. One of our ministers will come over to me after we have all finished. The minister reports how he has just had a great session with the usual several dozen demons cast out, manifestations, and healings taking place. This minister asks me if I wouldn't mind praying for him on some recent problems. We sit down and guess what? This minister manifests. Yet, he was just casting demons out of someone else!

This just goes to show how the Word really does perform itself as a **born again believer** speaks it. Even though we may not be a perfect vessel, we can still minister, and do it well. I say this to encourage you to step out with this understanding. And yes, we want to keep working on ourselves so our bodies and soul area (mind, will, emotions) do catch up with our born again, purified spirits.

There are hurting Christians all around us who never get the generational curses and other curses broken off, deliverance, inner-healing, physical healing, or the baptism of the Holy Spirit with speaking in tongues. The fact is, the bulk of Christians live their whole lives never enjoying the abundant life, the joy and the peace that was their inheritance. The need is much and the workers are few.

So by faith, go forth now as a believer doing the works of Jesus (John 14:12)
Following you will find:

- ✓ A two-page handout for everyone who comes for ministry
- ✓ A checklist for ministering to someone at your office or home
- ✓ A checklist for introduction to a group for one-on-one ministry and a "ministry report" checklist for individual ministry
- ✓ A checklist for ministry to a group or a mass deliverance

DELIVERANCE HANDOUT

FREE HANDOUT - PLEASE TAKE ONE

Our Authority – Door Openers – Breaking Ungodly Soul Ties – Keys for staying free

Our Authority:

Luke 10:19
"Behold, I give you the authority to trample on serpents and scorpions and over **ALL** the power of the enemy; and nothing shall by any means hurt you." (Memorize and quote daily)

Mark 16:17-18
"And these signs shall follow them that believe: In my name they shall cast out devils; they will speak with new tongues; they will take up serpents; and if they drink anything deadly, it will by no means hurt them; they will lay their hands on the sick, and they shall recover"

John 14:12
"I say unto you, anyone who believes in me, the works that I do; he shall do also; and greater works than these shall he do because I go to the Father."

How Christians are tormented by evil spirits...we have **three** parts. (1 Thessalonians 5:23) Our **spirit,** which is secure in Jesus, along with a **body** and a **soul** (mind, will, emotions), which can be tormented and influenced. The evil spirits are bothering Christians in the last two parts.

Door Openers:

1. **IGNORING THE NEED TO BE BORN AGAIN:** John 3:3; Romans 10:9-11, 10:13
2. **UNREPENTED SIN:** Proverbs 28:13, 1 John 1:9
3. **UNFORGIVENESS:** Mark 11:25-26; Matthew 18:34-35 Forgive others and ourselves. This is the BIG door opener! Unforgiveness is a major blockage to deliverance and healing. Jesus said if we don't forgive, we will be turned to the tormentors.
4. **HONOR YOUR FATHER AND MOTHER:** (So you will have long life and your life will go well) Deuteronomy 5:16; Ephesians 6:1-3
5. **WORKS OF THE FLESH:** Galatians 5:19-21; 2 Timothy 2:22
6. **PRIDE:** 1 Timothy 3:6; Proverbs 8:13

7. **WITCHCRAFT/SECRET SOCIETIES/FALSE RELIGIONS/YOGA:** Deuteronomy 18:10-14, Proverbs 18:21
8. **DRUGS, ALCOHOL:** Ephesians 4:27
9. **TRAUMA:** Emotional wounds of the past: being abused, severe fright, abandonment, rejection, neglect, tragedies, bad memories, (inner healing is needed.). Jesus renews our minds. Romans 12:2, Psalm 147:3, "He heals the broken hearted and binds up their wounds."
10. **HYPNOSIS:** When we are hypnotized, we yield our mind to others. Romans 6:16
11. **IDOLATRY:** Things, money, hobbies, job, relationships, drugs, alcohol, food, sports, etc. Exodus 20:3
12. **REBELLION AND DISOBEDIENCE TOWARD GOD:** Deuteronomy 28, 29, 30; Galatians 3:13
13. **INHERITANCE:** Confess and repent for the sins of the forefathers. Nehemiah 9:2
14. **CURSES:** By others, ourselves, or by oaths. Proverbs 18:21; Mark 11:23
15. **UNGODLY SOUL TIES:** 1 Samuel 18:1, Ephesians 4:27

Keys for staying free

Jesus used deliverance ministry to bring freedom to those oppressed by the devil. After being set free, paying careful attention to the following points will allow you to continue to live in freedom and maintain healing:

- Read the Word out loud each day. II Timothy 3:16-17
- Pray (talk to God conversationally) every day. Ephesians 6:18
- Have Christian fellowship. Matthew 18:19-20
- Keep the doors closed. Galatians 5:16-26
- Resist the devil, speaking the Word. James 4:7
- **Strengthen your spirit man** by **confessing or declaring daily** the positives, the Word of God and declaring the promises of God. Mark 11:22-25; Ephesians 1:3-23; 3:16-20
- Make godly choices. Deuteronomy 30:19

Then you will know the truth, and the truth will set you free. John 8:32

Breaking ungodly soul ties

Repeat the following:

1. Jesus, I forgive (<u>person's name</u>) for all that has happened, all that has gone on. Because You say that I must forgive to be forgiven, I make a decision to forgive (him/her). I forgive myself for the parts I may have

played here, and I ask You, Lord, to forgive me. I take any negative or tormenting feelings and unforgiveness that I carry toward ____, and I put these into my hands (Cup your hands together). Any hurts, bitterness, resentment, anger, offense, feelings of abandonment, betrayal, neglect, rejection, deception, manipulation, control. (Name any other negative emotions) So here they are, Lord; I give them to You. (Lift your hands up to Jesus and give them to Him. Certainly if we give them to Jesus, He will take them every time). *Cast all your anxiety on him because he cares for you 1 Peter 5:7.*

2. In Jesus' name, I also break the power of any curses _____ may have spoken over me. (If a parent, break generational curses.) I cancel any curses I might have spoken over ____ or myself. I cancel any ungodly vows that I may have made.

3. I also terminate, in Jesus' Name, any ungodly soul ties (I keep any godly ties) that exist between _____ and me. I do this spiritually, physically, mentally, emotionally, financially, (sexually if it applies) and I command any evil spirits that have come through these soul ties to depart, control spirit coming through _____, and any associated demon spirits to now go from me. Demons of the curses, in the name of Jesus, GO! (Stay engaged until you feel the spirits have departed.)

4. MINISTER: Ask the person to close their eyes and relax. Begin speaking to the person: Jesus, I think _____(name of person) needs some hugs. As Your child, Lord, would You put your arms around ____ and hold (him/her), comforting, assuring, loving and bringing Your truth to ____ so any lies that _____may have bought into and carried all these years can now be clarified. Your truth, Lord we ask… what You want ____to know.

(Now have them just sit there and listen. Sometimes they hear really well, others don't hear anything, but they seem to experience a peace that was not there before. It is obvious the Lord spoke into their spirit man with a healing.)

CHECKLIST FOR ONE-ON-ONE MINISTRY

(At your office or home)
DOOR CLOSING - SOUL TIES - INNER HEALING - DELIVERANCE

1. Try to determine how familiar they are with these works of Jesus. You might want to lead in with your testimony on how you were introduced into this type of ministry and how it can help Christians.
2. **Next, visit with them** to see what they would like to accomplish in the session. This step might take 15-30 minutes to get acquainted and to understand their over-all problems and needs. Hand out the problem list to fill out.
3. **Now the Deliverance handout**: Make sure they understand our authority (Luke 10:19) and how we Christians, in the Name of Jesus, have **ALL** power so they do not have any concerns about this type of ministry.
4. **Discuss the doors**: How we or our ancestors may have opened some of these doors for evil spirits to enter. How these spirits may have certain rights or roots that need to be cut. Explain that there is a door-closing prayer that should close the doors that the spirits may have used and how this usually makes ministry very easy.
5. Make sure there is an understanding of **how easy it is to recognize most evil spirits**. How you will know their names by what they are trying to do. The more compulsive a problem is, the more suspicious it is. (Note to the minister: I would suggest you mark the following groups even if they did not: bitterness, trauma, pain, condemnation, death, deception, destroyer, heaviness/stress, condemnation, satanic lies, rejection, torment/harassment, infirmities. Get specific on what infirmities...I like to do the infirmities last).
6. **Do the door-closing prayer**: You can take them through the prayer in Chapter 6 or let them follow the CD or DVD. Or, they can watch the DVD online at www.delmin.org. Give them plenty of time on unforgiveness.
7. **Do the soul tie prayers** with **inner healing, inner healing from birth up, work the problem list,** and finally command any remaining evil spirits to go, pray **physical healing**, put a seal on them by the Blood of Jesus. **Do the limb check. Administer the Baptism of the Holy Spirit** (see handout). **Point out the keys for staying free.**

CHECKLIST FOR GROUP INTRODUCTION

1. Hand out the "Problem List" to fill out when the people come in or in advance. Welcome the people and point out that this ministry will typically demonstrate the supernatural works of Jesus, using lay ministers who have gone through our training. These ministers are from many different churches. I usually read **Mark 16:17-20,** declaring that we will see signs following, or **Ephesians 6:11-12,** sometimes both.
2. Point out that there are **many Christians who have certain tormenting problems** (such as fear, anger, chronic depression, sickness), and while many have been seeking answers with doctors, professional or pastoral counseling, have been in prayer lines, victory has still not been achieved. I like to ask, "What good news would it be to find out by this type of ministry that often in one session, those kind of problems can be 'cast out' and those problems are gone! Would this be good news? Would the price be right? Yes, it is already paid for at the Cross."
3. **Give your testimony** on how you learned about the reality of this type of ministry. Some examples of what you have seen would be excellent. (On deliverance, inner healing, physical healing) I often touch on 1 Thessalonians 5:23, how we have three parts, that our spirits are secure in Jesus because we are born again Christians. However, evil spirits can torment us in our bodies and the soul area (mind, will, emotions) through oppression.
4. **Discuss how to recognize evil spirits** ... how the spirits tend to blow their cover by what they are trying to do (Examples of what you have seen). I usually mention that we typically see each person set free from around three dozen spirits, including infirmity spirits. The reason we know there are this many is that most people feel them coming out one at a time. Touching them with the Bible often helps to speed up the ministry. (Demons react as if the Bible is a burning sword.)
5. **Discuss the power** that Christians have (**Luke 10:17-19**). Suggest they memorize Luke 10:19 and quote it often out loud.
6. **Distribute the handout** and focus them on "**door openers.**" Explain that you will lead them through a 15-minute "repeat after me" prayer after the break that is designed to close these doors and cut the roots the enemy may have, generational curses, other curses or assignments. Go through these one at a time. Use examples as you are led. I usually mention that on #1, you must be born again or you don't get anywhere in all this. You have no power to stay free. On occasion someone may come who is not sure they are "born again." Point out that if they will sincerely repeat the sinner's prayer in the door closing that they will have the security of knowing that they are born again, or saved. I usually spend quite a bit of time on **unforgiveness** and how this is

a **major door for the tormentors (KJV Matthew 18:34-35)**, especially spirits of infirmity. They will have time to work on unforgiveness at the end of the door-closing prayer.

7. After the discussion on the doors, ask how many want ministry tonight ... get a show of hands. Receive the offering. **Hand out the problem list** (if they have not already filled it out) to those who want ministry. Point out you have pens and pencils on the table. There will be a 15-20 minute break, and you will be available during the break over at the table if they have some questions. Point out where the restrooms are located.
8. After the break, discuss each of the **keys for staying free** (on the handout). Point out as you **take them through the door-closing** prayer that people may experience some yawns, coughs or even burps. You may feel something stirring in the stomach area ... that's okay. Sometimes deliverance and healing may already be taking place during the door-closing prayer.
9. At the conclusion of the door-closing prayer, and as they are letting Jesus show them those they need to forgive, it is good, I think, to say something like, "**Tonight the Word has been sent to heal us and to deliver us from our destructions...and now in the Name of Jesus, I declare this place to be holy ground with supernatural signs following.**"
10. Give them at least 10-15 minutes to let Jesus show them who they need to forgive.
11. Place the ministers with the ones who want ministry.

CHECKLIST FOR A GROUP OR MASS DELIVERANCE

While I love the one-on-one method of ministry, there are situations where this is not possible. You may be at a church with only a few trained deliverance ministers with you, or perhaps not anyone with you. I have been invited to churches for mass deliverances with 100+ people there and have seen an amazing amount of relief take place, even physical healings. Don't underestimate the Holy Spirit!

1. Follow the "Format for group introduction," except adjusting as necessary since there will not be one-on-one ministry. (No individual interview)

   You will still be doing the main ministry steps:
   a. Some ungodly soul ties with inner healing
   b. Some inner healing from birth up
   c. All the list
   d. Commanding any remaining spirits to go
   e. Putting a seal on the people by the Blood
   f. Have an altar call for physical healing, including backs/necks, Baptism of the Holy Spirit. This can be done in a group.

2. When it is time for ministry, explain the first thing you are going to do is the breaking of ungodly soul ties three times. First you are going to do the **parents and any other relatives**. Explain that each person will need to say the names of the people when you say, "the names" in the prayer. Then take them through the ungodly soul tie prayer including inner healing at the end of each group.

   Next...the **sexual group**, including any **ex-spouses** and **present spouse**.

   Lastly, work **any others** on the soul tie list as a group, asking the people to put the names in as you lead them in the prayer.

3. Now minister inner healing from birth up. Tell them that you are going to ask Jesus to take them from birth up through the years, showing them any wounds connected with bad memories or events. Ask them to raise their hand as they lock onto something. (Probably not all of them will raise their hands...move on forward as you are led.) As they focus on a particular event, they may realize there are a lot of bad/tormenting feelings. Then, put those bad feelings into their hand; or if they can feel them balled up in their stomach or somewhere else, take

their hand, as a spiritual hand, to go inside, get their fingers around them, pull them out, and hand them up to Jesus.

Then ask Jesus to come and hug them as His child, comforting and speaking His truth about those relationships, so any lies they had carried can now be identified. Then wait a minute or so. You could ask for a show of hands on how many heard Jesus speak to them. Explain that even if they did not hear anything, since we asked Jesus to speak truth, He did speak into their spirit man and a supernatural peace always follows.

Ask Jesus to bring them on up to find another event, to raise their hand as they do. (In a mass deliverance, time will only allow you to do this several times.)

4. Explain that you are going to work all of the problem list now. You will start on the front page in the upper left and will go down. Tell them it is very important for them to engage their hearts with you, especially the ones that apply to them, commanding the possible spirits to go in Jesus' Name. Do not be passive. Take deep breaths, expelling anything that is in there. Touch their Bible on themselves as needed.

MINISTRY REPORT (After the Introduction and the door-closing prayer)

Date: _____

Minister's Name: _____

Person's Name: _____

Phone: _____ Email: _____

___ Introduction (introduce yourself and anyone sitting, in asking permission for someone to sit in.)
___ Begin your ministry with prayer. Ask the Holy Spirit to guide you. Quote Luke 10:19
___ Ask, "What does the person want to accomplish in the ministry session?"
___ **Interview:**
   what are the 1, 2 & 3 most tormenting areas? _____
   _____

   childhood, traumas? _____

   miscarriages? _____

   abortions? _____

   unresolved deaths? _____

   sexual abuse? _____

   witchcraft? _____

   freemasonry? _____

   physical needs? _____

   ex-spouses? _____

   sexual partners (sexual group)? _____

   How long was the interview? ____ minutes.

___ **Breaking Ungodly Soul Ties.** How many did you do? ___
Did you do mother, father and all spouses? Yes/No
Sexual group? Yes/No

___ Inner Healing: Did you do **inner healing after each of the Ungodly Soul Ties?** Yes/No

___ Did you do Charles Kraft's method of going back to conception and through the womb? Yes/No **Birth up? Yes/No**

___ Did you do A Simple Jesus Way of Healing Your Emotional & Mental Wounds. (Begins with present emotion and going back to the source as explained in chapter 8.) Yes/No **Any other type of inner healing?** Yes/No If yes what type?
_____

___ Deliverance with **problem list.** Were there manifestations? Yes/No What kind?
_____

___ Did you **fill them** with the Blood of Jesus as a seal? Yes/No

___ Did you **bless them?** Yes/No

___ **Physical Healing.** Yes/No If yes, what did you pray for?_____
_____

___ **Limb check/brain stem, C1, C2.** Yes/No If yes, what was the outcome?
_____
_____

___ **Baptism of the Holy Spirit?** Yes/No If yes, did they receive their prayer language? Yes/No Already had: Yes/No

What were the highlights of the ministry?_____
_____

Signed:_____

CHAPTER 16

STRANGE THINGS I HAVE SEEN DEMONS SAY AND DO

Since 1978, I have seen manifestations of demonic activity that many would never believe ... only a fraction of one percent of the Christian body is privy to the reality of this taking place.

Some Christians say that we should not be interrogating demons. Jesus did. Look at Mark 5:9, where Jesus interrogated the "demoniac" at the tombs in the Gadarenes. Jesus said, "What is your name?" And he answered, saying, "My name is Legion: for we are many." Jesus negotiated with the demons as the conversation continued, sending the demons into the swine that were nearby. Christians must always keep in mind John 14:12, that we are to be doing the same works of Jesus, even "greater works."

Now, we know that Satan is a great deceiver (Revelation 13:14) and a liar (John 8:44), so we must always be on guard. Here is something that we have found really works well ... when a demon tells you something, say right back to it, "Will you confess what you just told me to be true before the Lord Jesus Christ and the Holy Spirit?" The demon will answer back yes or no to that question. If you catch it lying, then you can call on God's warring angels (Hebrew 1:14) to discipline the demon with several jabs with their swords. That will usually keep the demons in line. Sometimes we have to get more severe.

My experience is we (including our trained ministers) will see demons speak out of the Christians' mouths only about a third of the time. The majority of the others will feel the evil spirits coming out, often with yawns, coughs or burps. I have had to conclude that everyone is just different in their sensitivities to the spirit world. We have noted that with about 10% of the vocal manifestations, the person was not aware of what was happening. The demons were talking and in full control. The person had no clue what was going on.

THESE ARE SOME OF THE STRANGE THINGS WE HAVE SEEN DEMONS SAY AND DO:

- A procrastination spirit said: "Let's put this off to tomorrow."
- A gluttony spirit in a 50-year-old man said: "There goes my meal ticket."
- At the end of a deliverance session, especially if there were vocal manifestations, I often command any spirits remaining to present themselves, front and center. Out of one person's mouth came: "There aren't any more of us in here." In another case, when asked the question, back came a voice that said, "We are all gone now." (It seems that some demons are not very smart, and yet other times they will run us around in circles).
- A demon announced, in a man who was about 25 years old, that its name was "driving." I thought perhaps it was a workaholic spirit that was driving him, but when I asked it how it was doing its mission, it said: "I cause him to have fun driving." I drew it out some more with more questions, "I cause him to drive too fast." It finally came to me ... this is a "driving of a car" spirit! As we broke its assignment off of him and commanded the spirit of "driving, fun driving and driving too fast" to come out, the man manifested as he sat in his chair and was squirming. Then his arms started straightening out, his hands pretending he was holding onto a steering wheel! And if I had thought to look, more than likely his right foot was pushed hard against the floor! You can see how the demon of death could be involved here, driving this man to his death. It was not long after this that I was visiting with a woman who told me that her best friend had just lost her daughter the previous weekend in a car wreck. The woman said, "You know, that girl always had a tendency to drive too fast. Her car went out of control and rolled ... she was by herself." I thought ... you don't suppose it was another driving too fast demon? In this case, the demon accomplished its assignment.
- I'm not surprised at anything anymore: I was asked to minister to a woman who was in the choir of an Episcopal church and primarily had an alcohol problem. I had gone to school with the head priest. He knew I was in the deliverance ministry, so he asked me to minister to her one evening after the choir practice. We went to a side room, began ministry, and she began to manifest. I cast out a number of spirits, including a generational alcohol spirit. Finally, I was calling up anything else that was still there to speak up, in Jesus' Name. This voice came up and gave its name as "Cold." Initially, I thought it might be coldness toward people, but it finally said, "I'm the spirit that keeps her cold all the time." I realized this was a physical cold

spirit. When I cast it out, the woman suddenly said, "Oh, I feel this heat on my back." I thought it might be the Holy Spirit on her, but then it occurred to me, it was just the absence of cold. Since then, I have run into other spirits of cold, even spirits of "hot." What else is out there?

- I remember a nicotine spirit manifesting in a woman. It took her hand with her fingers pretending she was holding a cigarette and blowing smoke.
- A rather dignified-looking woman with black hair manifested a generational Indian "war dance spirit." She was sitting in a chair, her hand came up to her mouth, and using the palm of her hand started making Indian dance sounds. Her feet also started going up and down like she was doing a dance. Of course, that all quit after the spirit was cast out. She did not appear to have any Native American in her bloodlines, except possibly her black hair. We broke off any inherited spirits.
- I'll never forget this one: (I even found my old notes) It was in October of 1980 and I was ministering to a surgical nurse. We had just finished ministering to her friend, where a rather violent suicide spirit had been cast out, as well as a couple of dozen other spirits. She told me, "When you were ministering with my friend, I felt like there was something inside me, will you minister to me?" Much to my surprise, she had more vocal manifestations than her friend. One announced its name as "poverty." Then it began a chant, "I want to keep her poor, I want to keep her poor so she can't give to that old church, I want to keep her poor." I thought, "That sounds like Satan. If he can keep Christians poor, they can't give much." Through the years, we have seen this to be a rather common spirit – it is normally there by a curse or satanic assignment.
- I've spoken at 56 of the Full Gospel Businessmen Fellowship International Banquets through the years. The people came to hear a nice mortgage banker give his testimony. I have always had an altar call for everything, including deliverance. This happened in three of those banquets: Spirits of suicide manifested, giving their names, and then their own hands went up to their throats and started choking themselves. People gasped. My daughter, Marla, was with me twice in the prayer line when these happened. She reached up, grabbed the wrists and tried to pull the choking hands loose, but there seemed to be a supernatural physical strength. I said, "In Jesus' Name, violence be still." Then, the hands released. What a <u>demonstration</u> of the power we have in His Name!
- At another Full Gospel Business Men's Fellowship banquet in Fayetteville, Arkansas, in the early 80s, we all saw an amazing thing

happen. A young woman started manifesting in the prayer line, so I had her sit down in a chair off to the side and told her I would finish the line and come back to her. We found out she had a lesbian problem. When we addressed it, she flipped forward up in the air and came facedown on the floor. We all looked at each other and wondered, "How did she do that!" The spirit was finally cast out.

- At a cafeteria meeting room in McAlester, Oklahoma, the Full Gospel Business Men's chapter had invited me to give my testimony. I had the usual altar call without doing the door-closing prayer (I always do it today). A woman in the prayer line had a demon identify itself as an antichrist spirit. It suddenly went into the loudest scream that you can imagine, so loud that I had to get up in her ear and yell as loud as I could at the top of my lungs, "In Jesus' Name, be still!" It finally got quiet and I was able to continue in ministry. I've always wondered what those people in the front of the cafeteria thought was happening at the "Business Men's meeting."

- I remember a similar screamer, that happened at my mortgage office one evening. To make light of the situation, I have always jokingly told our employees if they took a loan application after hours on a Monday night, something might be heard from my side of the office as we minister. Just to tell the customer, "Don't be alarmed, it's just our collection department. Someone must have missed a payment." (We always had an excellent collection record).

- In another case, a witchcraft spirit was manifesting in a young woman. When we said the name of Jesus, it said, "I don't like that name." It also reported, "We have more power." (They don't say that again after you quote Luke 10:19!) Then it said, "She's mine, she's mine, we mean you no harm, she's mine." (My comment, "Yeah, right".) When we laid the Bible against her back, it yelled, "It's burning, it's burning." Witchcraft finally left!

- A woman, 34 years old, came to my office with her husband. Both were attorneys. She stated that one of her problems was that she did not have any energy, either to do her legal work or to maintain the home and her three-year-old daughter. When we got into ministry, she manifested, bent over my conference table with a pain in her stomach, and this voice said its name was "old and tired." (I have since added it to the fatigue and tiredness group.) Her husband was sitting there, watching with big eyes. I'm sure he was in shock. As soon as it was cast out, she felt more energy! Sounds like the enemy, doesn't it? If Satan can keep the Christians tired all the time, we won't feel like reading the Word, doing our ministries, or being able to work for the abundant life. A couple of weeks later, her little three-year-old came up to her and said, "Mommy, I feel real tired."

The mother thought, "You don't suppose?" She commanded the spirit of old and tired to come out. Immediately the little girl said, "I feel it in my tummy." Then her daughter yawned a big yawn and the spirit was gone. The mother said her little girl has never had the problem after that. What is also amazing about this case is that the mother's mother came in for ministry a few weeks later and we discovered that she also had "old and tired." Three generations of this demon. We know by experience that the sins of the fathers (mothers) are visited upon their children to the third and fourth generation. The mother/attorney was a guest on my radio show and gave her testimony about all of this. That interview can also be heard on the Deliverance Ministries website: www.delmin.org. The tired, fatigue, old and tired group is more common than we have thought. The reason this assignment is on many Christians is obvious … a tired Christian can't do much. Recently, at a pastor's luncheon, a brother next to me complained of being tired all the time. I shared with him about my experience with this spirit. We broke its assignment off of him and rebuked it. He felt energized immediately! I see him each week; he is amazed at the difference.

- A young lady accompanied by her parents came to Oklahoma City from Dallas with an anorexia problem. They were convinced it was demonic because she kept hearing voices. When she began to eat with a fork, a voice would say, "Don't pick up that fork or we will punish you." She had told her parents to be ready to call 911 when she got to my office, as the voices had told her they were going to kill her if she went for ministry. Funny, during the deliverance, the spirits were as quiet as a mouse. After ministry, she said to us, "I feel hungry!" During the following week at her home, the demons did make one last stand. They manifested, talking out of her mouth, but this time the parents and the young lady rebuked the spirits in warfare … she was set free!
- There was a man who came to my office for ministry. He had about 40 evil spirits and every one of them talked. It was a classic manifestation case. Since I record my radio interview show there and my equipment was right next to us, I put a tape in, set the mike on the table and continued the session. As it turned out, I got about half of the deliverance recorded. He gave me permission later to use the recording for teaching purposes. One of the demons was manifesting but not coming out. So I said to it, "You are going to get the Word." The spirit, glaring through the man's eyes with a concerned look, finally said, "No, not the Word." I quickly said back, "Yes, you are getting the Word." I then took one end of the Bible and stuck it gently right against his belly. This gurgling sound then came out of

his mouth, similar to what you would expect to hear if you were sticking a person with a sword. At that point, the demon was gone. We read in Ephesians 6:17 that the Word of God is the sword of the Spirit. This must be how the evil spirits see it. Our anointed Word is awesome! "The Word of God is quick and powerful, sharper than a two-edged sword."

CHAPTER 17

ADDITIONAL THOUGHTS AND OBSERVATIONS

ONLY ONE WAY

You hear people say they believe that many religions have a pathway to God, salvation, and eternal life in Heaven. Even Oprah Winfrey says it. After all, other religions seem to have their own Bible and books. Why should the Christian Bible be any different?

Here is why:

For thousands of years, prophets of God gave detailed prophecies of the Messiah who was to come and who would be the final sacrificial lamb for mankind and man's sin. These were recorded in the Old Testament. In fact, one of my Bibles lays these prophecies out in chronological order. The prophecies of the Old Testament and the fulfillment as recorded in the New Testament. **Thirty-seven** of them, including the resurrection, and **Jesus fulfilled them all!** What are the mathematical odds of these happening by accident? A PhD in mathematics was asked the question, "Do you believe in the God of the Bible?" He said, "I am a mathematician. Statistically, I have to believe."

If this leads us to the point of believing that the Bible is true, then we would probably want to know what it says; especially in what was recorded about Jesus and what is contained in the New Testament.

Jesus made very clear statements. "I am the way, the truth, and the life. No one comes to the Father but by me" (John 14:6). Jesus also said, "I and my Father are one" (John 10:30).

It gets down to this … people are going to have to accept what He said or they are going to have to call Jesus a liar.

The New Testament is overwhelming in making the point that Jesus is the only way:

"Neither is there salvation in any other: for there is none other name under heaven given among men, whereby we must be saved" (Act 4:12).

"For there is one God, and one mediator between God and men, the man Christ Jesus." (1Timothy 2:5)

"And this is the record, that God hath given us eternal life, and this life is in his Son. He that has the Son has life: and he that hath not the Son of God hath not life." (1 John 5:11-12)

If you love the people around you and care about them, would you not want them to know the truth? It's too important to miss.

Remember one thing: Jesus is the only religious leader in all of history who went to hell and took the keys of death, hell, and the grave from Satan himself. He was raised from the dead by the power of the Holy Spirit, and is alive today, seated at the right hand of God Almighty. All other religious leaders occupy their graves.

"HIS DAD CAST IT OUT"

Last week, a young born again Christian named Roger called and reminded me that eight years ago, he was set free from drugs and alcohol and has been free ever since! We discussed how the Jesus way is the easy way. We desire that more Christians understood this.

The deliverance with Roger started with his dad. I remember the story well. This particular night, Roger was at home when the demons oppressing him became violent and threw him against the wall. His father saw this and went online to find a web site to give some basic information on exorcisms. With the instructions in hand, his dad commanded various spirits to leave his son. Roger calmed down and felt better. However, Roger's friend heard the radio interview program of Deliverance Ministries and suggested that Roger attend a Monday evening session to be sure that he was completely free.

The evening that Roger came, another lay minister, John Sigmon of Norman, and I ministered to Roger with interesting results. We were able to get the head demon up, interrogating it as for the demonic structure under its authority. We were focusing on understanding the department heads in authority below this head demon, and how many demons were in each department. We also were demanding from the head demon to tell us if there were any remaining legal rights for any of the demons to be able to stay, tormenting Roger. We wanted to make sure that the legal rights had been cancelled. We recorded all of this on a yellow tablet. Even though drugs were listed, I noticed that alcohol was not on listed. We knew from the initial interview with Roger that alcohol had been one of his major problems.

When we inquired of the head demon, "What about the spirit of alcohol?" The head demon reported, "His dad cast it out!"

When Christians speak in the Name of Jesus… the power goes forth (Luke 10:17-19)!

THE DECEIVER IS AT WORK

I ministered to two different Christian ladies who had been listening to the deceiver for quite some time, thinking it was God or the Holy Spirit speaking to them. This experience seems to be quite common in the body of Christ.

Revelations 11:9 tells us, **"Satan deceives the whole world."**

Through the years, I have heard Christians say, "The Lord told me this or that." Certainly the Lord does speak to people. Some people have the gift of prophecy. **If someone has that gift and is sensitive to the spirit world, it is reasonable to believe that they would be able to hear both sides (Holy Spirit and evil spirits).** That is why it is so important to have a foundation in the Word of God; i.e., believing and speaking the Word of truth. We need to test every thought to make sure that it lines up with the scriptures.

We need to interrogate every voice we hear, according to 1 John 4:1-3, "Will you confess that Jesus Christ has come in the flesh?" If it says no, you can be assured it is a demon. If it says yes, then question it right back with, "Jesus, the Christ who arose on the third day?" That should pin it down, but if the answer is not clear, ask if it is a demon. If it says no, then say to it, "Will you confess what you just told me to be true before the Lord Jesus Christ and the Holy Spirit?" You will know then who it is that speaking to you.

I spoke at the Full Gospel Business Men's Fellowship banquet in Salina, Kansas several years ago. A man came up to me with a sad story. A voice spoke to him one night. He thought it was an angel that told him to sell the farm and move to Africa. He did this and fell flat on his face, finally losing all his money. At the time, he did not know how to interrogate the voice by 1 John 4.

In each of the two ladies I mentioned before, I was able to get the head demon up. I had the demons disclose the top lies they were speaking into their minds. I was amazed how parallel these lies were … and these two women did not even know each other and were not in on each other's ministry sessions.

Here were some of the lies:

LADY A
"It is I that speaketh ... the Lord God."
"You are to do this and that."
"Give away all your worldly possessions."
"I make the rules and punishment comes from me if she disobeys."
"I cause her to mutilate herself and overdose."
"Cut her throat."
"She is not worthy."
"I told her lies to make her love me."

I said to the demon, "Is she buying into the lies?" It said, "Oh yes, we are doing so good." And laughed.

The demon also told me "She loves me and will never want me to go." I told it, "She knows who you are now, that means your deception is over!" It let out a squeal.

The head demon was the deceiver with the usual three dozen lesser demons. There were two groups of fear. Also included in the list of demons were poverty, suicide, depression, and loneliness.

LADY B
"I am the Holy Ghost."
"I am God."
"I forced her to put mucus on her face."
"Do not talk to her family."
"I told her the dog was healed." (It was a lie)
"I told her that her back was healed." (It was a lie)
"Take money out of her retirement fund."
"She needs to sell the truck."
"She needs to buy more clothes."
"I influenced her to say things so she would not be hired."
"I told her that her dad died because of her."

It also said there was a program to block her memory, to control her, to drive her crazy, to cause pain in her back, and to block her immune system. The spirit of poverty made her spend all her money. It caused her dog to die. Strangely enough, when fear would manifest it brought an unusual odor.

The head demon was tormentor, and deceiver was the executive officer. (The deceiver was the spokesman for all of the lesser ranking demons.) The usual three dozen lesser demons included rejection and rebellion. Confusion said that he had done a job on her.

The bulk of the demons were there by satanic assignments. Both ladies had to repent of accepting the voices and renounce them to break the demons' legal right to torment them.

WE CAN SPEAK DIRECTLY TO IT!

Most of us who grew up in church got the message that when we pray, we should always pray to the Father in Jesus' Name or pray to Jesus (John 16:23 & John 14:13). And yes, prayers are answered this way.

We also find that we, as born again Christians, can speak **directly** to our situations. Just as Jesus spoke directly to the fig tree and it dried up at its roots; He spoke to the storm at Galilee and it became still; **Jesus commanded believers to do His same works in His name** (John 14:12).

When we are casting out demons from someone, we find it works quite well to speak **directly** to the demons to come out, in the name of Jesus … and they do!

Jesus quite clearly made a point of this in Mark 11:23, when He said to speak **directly** to the mountain and it will be removed and cast into the sea.

For many years, we thought we needed to go through the Godhead to ask the angels' help in demonic warfare. Someone finally pointed out to me that I can speak **directly** to the angels (Hebrews 1:14). Today, whenever a manifesting demon starts getting physical, I call on the angels directly to hold the person, and they do.

We had a lady at our Monday evening ministry session who was starting to get violent; in fact, her husband was trying to hold her arms. I told him, "Let the angels hold her." I called on the angels **directly** to hold her in the chair, and, they did. She was unable to move her arms. We continued the deliverance with great freedom following.

I have seen over three decades of backs and necks getting healed as we speak **directly** to the problem. So often we see that there is a short leg or arm as a result of being out of adjustment. Usually, all I have to say is, "In Jesus' Name, adjust, pain go." and we watch the short leg or arm come out and equal the other. When the people check themselves out, the pain is gone. **What awesome power we have as we speak directly to our issues in the Name of Jesus.**

So the question is: What should we be speaking directly to in our lives … our health, our finances, our relationships? What?

MOST CHRISTIANS ARE BOTHERED BY DEMONS

Strong statement? I'm not saying we are possessed in our born again spirits, but rather harassed and tormented in our bodies and soul area (mind, will, emotions).

Have you ever known of a sick Christian? Ever known of a Christian with a fear or anger problem? How about chronic stress and depression? Addictions?

For 30 years now, I have seen the above evil spirits cast out (and many more) of born again, Spirit-filled Christians. Most Christians think these are flesh and blood problems; i.e., problems that are psychological or physical. Most seek answers with drugs and therapy, just like the rest of the unsaved world.

Paul warned the church that we wrestle not against flesh and blood but against the demonic (Eph. 6:10-18). It's certainly as true today as it was then. The point is driven home when you see demons speak out of a Christian's mouth and say their master is Satan.

Why do you think Jesus so clearly commanded believers to cast out demons (Mark 16:17)? Because most Christians have them! We typically see around three dozen evil spirits cast out by the end of a ministry session. It's no wonder people we minister to feel so wonderful when they leave.

You might say, "Well, how do you know you get that many demons out of someone?" Because most people feel them physically depart! When any one spirit leaves, the person feels a little better.

To me, getting deliverance is a lot like getting in a hot shower. These parasite-like things are washed away, and guess who is left? The real person who is made in God's image with special gifts and talents, and is now able to go forward unhindered by tormenting evil spirits.

What saddens me is that most Christians live their whole lives tormented by these things, when the answer was right under their nose. They never achieve their destinies and are certainly not living the abundant life.

Jesus is ready when the person is ready!

WHO DO YOU KNOW WHO NEEDS A JESUS OVERHAUL?

There are so many **Christians who are tormented ...** look at your relatives, your friends, your neighbors, people you work with, including some of your church friends who are struggling. **Many have issues with fear, panic attacks, anger and rage, chronic stress, depression and anxiety, addictions to nicotine, cocaine, gambling or pornography.** Even more have illnesses that may be a **spirit of infirmity** (Luke 3:11).

Each Monday evening (except major holidays) from 5:30-9:30, people get set free from the above and much more! We see mental and physical healings.

A typical Monday evening one-on-one ministry session:

Introduction to this works of Jesus and a Christian's authority
A discussion of the doors that evil spirits often use to enter
The 15-minute door-closing prayer, then one-on-one ministry
Breaking of ungodly soul ties with inner healing of that relationship
Healing of emotional wounds of the past

Deliverance
Physical healing prayer
How to stay free and healed
Baptism of the Holy Spirit

Jesus is ready if you are!

CHAPTER 18

PROOF OF THE PUDDING – TESTIMONIES

For the last 32 years, I have seen miracles happen before my eyes that most believers would be astonished to see. Jesus is still setting the captives free in the 21st Century. One of my favorite scriptures is Acts 10:38, "God anointed Jesus of Nazareth with the Holy Spirit and with power, who went about doing good and healing all who were oppressed by the devil, for God was with Him." We have taken the time to work with many individuals who have been tormented and discouraged by many issues that have not been helped by counseling and prayer ministry in the local church. After years of counseling and the laying on of hands, nothing has changed. People who are tormented come to us as a last resort. They are desperate for something that will make a difference. The testimonies I have included in this chapter are actual people who have seen their lives changed by the living Jesus who cares for them and continues to set the captives free. These testimonies are about their freedom.

The reason I did the radio interview show for 22 years was to press this point that the same things that went on in the ministry of Jesus and the New Testament are happening today. **Christians** are getting set free of many of their problems and healed … often in one session of a few hours.

**The following are summaries of some of the interviews
I aired on the radio during those 22 years:**
(You can hear some of these testimonies on the ministry web site:
www.delmin.org)

Panic Attacks

Vanessa, a beautiful, born again, Spirit-filled young lady of 25, was tormented with panic attacks. This had been going on since she was 15. These anxiety attacks were coming upon her several times a day. She told me she couldn't even go out to eat anymore because of the panic attacks. She could not even date. Her life was miserable. She had tried numerous medications and professional counseling. She said her skin color would turn a bright red during these panic attacks. The minister who worked with her was able to find a root cause. Vanessa had been embarrassed in the sixth grade by a teacher. Unforgiveness had opened the door to a demonic attack of her emotions. Forgiveness, breaking an ungodly soul tie with this teacher, and inner healing closed this door forever. In addition to other spirits of darkness that harassed her, she was successfully delivered from panic attacks, depression, laziness and a spirit of embarrassment. She is no longer oppressed and harassed. She has the freedom to live a normal life as a Spirit-filled, faithful Christian. She was able to date and eventually was married because of the freedom she experienced!

Fear

Lee had been born again and filled with the Spirit of God for 16 years before she came to us and received ministry. She was especially tormented with fear. Not surprisingly, she was fearful about coming for deliverance, but finally came because some of her Christian friends supported her. She reported this anxiety would come upon her at night when she would try to go to sleep. After we began the process of ministry, it became obvious there was a lot of generational fear coming against her. Fear had been a major problem with her ancestors for many generations back. The power of God and Jesus' Name broke the generational curses. During the session, several dozen spirits, including more than one spirit of fear, were commanded to go. Lee reported that she shuddered physically as the spirits came out. When all of them were gone an "immediate" change took place in her life! Jesus set her free. We interviewed her seven months later and she reported to the public on our radio program that she was still free.

Fear of Flying

Gloria had been born again and filled with the Holy Spirit for a period of 14 years. She was a strong, active Christian in her church. She came to us for ministry because she had an airplane trip coming up and wanted to deal with claustrophobia before the trip. She also had a fear of flying. In addition, Gloria was tormented with other fears: fear of the dark, insecurity and various other tormenting spirits. She was puzzled that a Spirit-filled Christian like her could be bothered like this ... that she had not been taught how to get free. As we started into ministry, the spirit of fear caused numbness in her throat as well as a choking sensation. The two ladies who ministered to her commanded the spirit of fear to come out, placing a Bible on her throat to help expel this demon of fear. Finally, the spirit departed and she felt relieved. When I interviewed her four months later, Gloria expressed how she enjoyed the airplane trip and is now sleeping with the light off after receiving such awesome ministry in Jesus Name!

Fear/Insomnia

Marge's dad died when she was very young. After the death of her father, she found that she could not sleep well because of fear. It got worse and worse over time, to the point that she had a nervous breakdown. When she was hospitalized, her life got worse because of all the medications the doctors were prescribing. She developed a smoking habit and experienced migraine headaches. During this period of time, she saw a vision from God. She would see Jesus with His arms reaching out to her even though she was not born again. After she was released from the hospital, she asked a local minister to pray for her to surrender her life to Jesus! The minister asked her to raise her hands and thank the Lord for coming into her life. Suddenly, she started speaking in tongues. However, as time passed, Marge continued to be tormented with many fears. Sometimes these spirits would physically tug on her clothes! Marge heard of a local Christian who was skilled in deliverance ministry. There she received her victory from fear, tranquilizers, and the migraine headaches. She did share with us that later on, the demons of fear and headache that tormented her for so many years tried to come back. But, she had learned how to resist the devil in Jesus' Name! Seventeen years had passed since her deliverance when I interviewed her. She is still free!!! Praise Jesus. He is so wonderful!

Fear/Wrath

Jenny was born again at the age of seven, and received the baptism of the Holy Spirit some years later. She was very active in her church. She came to

Deliverance Ministries to support her husband. On the evening she heard the introduction on these works of Jesus, she decided she might have some evil spirits bothering her. Jenny looked at the problem list and circled fear, pride, strife and numerous others ... she had just not recognized them as major problems before. After the door-closing prayer, the breaking of ungodly soul ties and inner healing from past emotional wounds, the team who ministered to her began to hear a spirit of "wrath" identify itself by speaking through her. When I interviewed her, she explained that spirit moved inside of her body from her left leg to her stomach and finally to her right hand. These were sensations she felt in her physical body during the deliverance. The team put a Bible on her right hand and commanded the spirit to go to the feet of Jesus, in Jesus' Name. "The spirit had to pack up and leave." She went through some coughing as she expelled the demons. Jenny said, "A big key to my deliverance was forgiving everyone and especially myself." She is now able to go everywhere without fear and has a strong self-identity and God identity that she never had before. Praise God!!!

Seizures

Both Jim A. and his younger sister were tormented with seizures. Jim had been experiencing them since he was 15, and his sister experienced seizures since she was six. Doctors were puzzled, as brain scans did not show any physical reasons for the problems. After coming to receive deliverance and break generational curses, both of them stopped experiencing seizures. They were still free from any seizures after two years. Jesus is still in the miracle-working business.

Healed of Crohn's Disease

Stephanie was tormented with Crohn's Disease, which attacks the colon. She had been diagnosed with Crohn's Disease when she was 15. She was 26 at the time of the deliverance. She could not work and had difficulty attending college. She couldn't maintain her weight. Her normal weight was between 125 to 130, but she only weighed 92 pounds. Stephanie found that she had to do some forgiving of people. She completed the process of forgiving by choosing to forgive herself. We commanded a spirit of infirmity and Crohn's to go to the feet of Jesus for judgment. She said she could feel something physical happening in her stomach, moving to the top of her head, finally coming out the top of her head. Other spirits were cast out. When they left, she yawned as much as her mouth would allow. Stephanie said she had been skeptical when she came, but found she received healing through deliverance of evil spirits that attacked her emotions, her mind and her body. Her weight is now up to 117. She shares her exciting testimony with others, letting them know that there is hope in Jesus.

Heart Attack Spirit

Pastor James of Carlsbad, New Mexico reported an astonishing deliverance that took place there. He was at home one afternoon and received a call from a housewife saying she had just talked to her husband, who was in great pain. He told her instead of heading to the hospital, he was driving to Pastor James' house for prayer. She said she was greatly concerned about him. There were several members of the church at the house when he arrived. They started looking down the street and finally saw him coming down the road with the car weaving and jumping the curb, landing in the yard of Pastor James. They ran out to the car and found this husband slumped over the steering wheel, gasping, saying, "I can't breathe." As they took him into the house, someone called 911. Then he lost color in his face and passed out. They could not feel a pulse. The group of believers started praying. Then, Pastor James heard the Lord say, "This man does not need prayer, he needs deliverance, cast out the spirit." They began commanding the spirit to come out. Suddenly, the man lurched forward and a voice spoke out of him saying, "No! I came in to destroy him ... he will never preach. Ha, ha, ha." (Pastor James said he had been scheduled to preach his first sermon the very next week). When the spirit had been cast out, the man's color returned, his pulse became normal and the pain was gone. The man then said, "Thank God I had someone treating me who knew what to do."

Back Pain/Neck

Dr. John is a chiropractor, born again and Spirit-filled. He felt the Lord had told him that Satan was coming against him and his business. For five years he had been tormented with pain in his neck, in his back and head. This pain had been constant and tormented him on a daily basis. When he came for ministry, he said he felt something churning in his stomach as this part of the gospel was discussed. As he received ministry, he felt the evil spirits moving around physically in his back and neck. Today, he is free and feels "fantastic." Dr. John has been surprised how he has such a hunger for the Word now. He spends more time than ever before reading and meditating on the Word of God, with great joy. He recommends this type of ministry for anyone.

Thyroid/Deafness/Generational Witchcraft

Betty was born again as a child and had received the Baptism of the Holy Spirit six years before receiving deliverance ministry. She came for ministry previously and had been healed of a thyroid problem. She commented about the doctors running two tests on her thyroid. They finally conceded that her thyroid was healed. Much later, Betty had another ministry session with us because she was bothered with "heaviness" in her right ear. This experience had gone on for six months. She couldn't hear people behind her. This was especially tormenting. In ministry, the spirit of deafness manifested, throwing her head back and forth. When the spirit came out, her hearing was "greatly improved." Also, a spirit of witchcraft manifested during the deliverance session, speaking in a Welsh dialect, which she did not understand. (Betty has Welsh in her ancestral lines.) Furthermore, her grandfather read tea leaves for guidance. The grandfather's reading of tea leaves was the door he opened for the witchcraft spirit to enter her life. A spirit of rejection spoke out and admitted it came in when her father had left home, abandoning her and her mother when she was a young child. Betty was healed of this abandonment through inner healing. We also cast out the spirit of rejection as well as other evil spirits. When a spirit of nervousness was cast out, she experienced a severe shaking. Betty received a Jesus overhaul, making life so much better for her.

Migraine Headaches

Jamie was born again when she was eight years old and was raised in church. When Jamie came to us for ministry, she had been experiencing migraine headaches weekly for ten years. Her family suggested she look into deliverance, since nothing else had made any difference at all. She listened to the introduction on how to recognize possible evil spirits and the doors the spirits often use to enter our lives. She found out that she did have some unforgiveness. (We all need to forgive quickly and often.) Jamie was surprised how easy the ministry went. She actually felt the spirits leave physically. She reported how it was somewhat difficult to breathe just before a spirit would leave. And, she kept feeling better and better, and "lighter and lighter." Over the next few weeks, she started realizing how much had really happened. The anxiety and insomnia were gone, and best of all, no more migraine headaches! I interviewed her five weeks later and she was still free. Thank You, Jesus. You are so wonderful to set the captives free today.

"I saw demons in my room."

Lee Ann was not born again yet and was eight months pregnant when a friend invited her to go to a palm reader. At the palm reading, Lee Ann felt uneasy, especially when she heard about the future doom and gloom the palmist shared. Years later, Lee Ann became born again and filled with the Holy Spirit and life seemed good. However, her daughter was seeing demons in her room at night. One demon in particular would stand in her doorway, terrifying her. At the age of 15, her daughter received Jesus into her heart and the Baptism of the Holy Spirit; however, her daughter still had a lot of fear troubling her. It was a number of years later, during a church meeting, that a fear spirit manifested by speaking out of her mouth, right there in church! Lee Ann and her daughter scheduled an appointment and came to Deliverance Ministries a few days later. In this ministry session, the spirit of fear spoke through her daughter and admitted it had come in through the palm reader (a door she opened to demonic oppression). That door was closed by repenting and renouncing visiting the palm reader. Then, the spirit of fear was cast out. Today, the daughter is a minister of the gospel.

Eleven-year-old Son Tormented

Mory told how he and his wife, Debbie, had taken their eleven-year-old son to numerous neurologists in Oklahoma City and eventually to the Mayo Clinic in Minneapolis for tests. They were trying to find out the cause of his "tics," an involuntary physical jerking with vocal sounds. The clinic came up with many different possibilities; however, no medical treatment made any difference for their son. There is no treatment for "tics." It was ultimately determined that Pokemon and a card game that would summon up evil spirits was opening the door to the supernatural demonic realm, allowing spirits of darkness to torment their son with "tics." The Pokemon and card game were removed from the house in an attempt to close the door to this spirit realm. During the ministry the son received, he felt the demons moving out of his legs, upward in his body. As we touched him with the Bible in areas where he felt them moving, they finally come out as he yawned several times. The father reported in an interview, more than six months after the ministry time, that the "tics" have vanished without any medication.

Grand Mal Seizures

Anita brought her daughter, who was in her first year of college, to Deliverance Ministries. She came because she was experiencing grand mal seizures. Anita and her daughter were part of a Christian family attending a denominational church that seemed to avoid teaching and ministering in this part of the Gospel. Nevertheless, Anita had a friend who knew of Deliverance Ministries and suggested this type of ministry might help. Prior to considering Deliverance Ministries, they had been to four different neurologists, as well as to the Mayo Clinic for diagnosis and treatment. The medical report called it non-medical seizures. Consequently, there was no treatment available. Anita said that it reminded her of the passage in Mark 9 where a spirit would try to throw the child into the fire or water. In her daughter's case, her daughter's head would be thrown against the headboard of the bed. At other times, it seemed as though something or someone was attempting to throwing her down the stairs. Anita heard a low, guttural voice coming out of her daughter. This scared her. When we proceeded into ministry, a head demon manifested. This head demon said that its name was "destroyer." As we interrogated this demon, destroyer stated that it was there under a satanic assignment to block her life. We know that Jesus said that the devil came to kill, steal and destroy; however, Jesus came to bring life and life more abundantly (John 10.10). Anita said she was amazed at how many spirits were cast out of her daughter. These spirits' names included suicide and anger. A total of 38 that were cast out, including the head demon as the last demon to be cast out. We sent these spirits to the feet of Jesus, never to harm anyone in the future. As we interviewed Anita nine months later, we discovered that her daughter no longer had seizures and was anxious to graduate and minister the Gospel of Jesus Christ. As she is launched into ministry, this daughter of the King will have nothing holding her back from doing the works of Jesus.

Old and Tired

Carrie, a practicing attorney, and her husband came to Deliverance Ministries seeking relief from various infirmities, including chronic fatigue. As a born again Christian and filled with the Holy Spirit, Carrie knew she was not experiencing the abundant life she was promised by God. She had no energy to care for her two small children and do her legal work. Once we began ministry, a voice spoke out of Carrie's mouth and announced its name as "old and tired." The voice even sounded old. As the spirit departed, Carrie gagged, and almost threw up. She told me in the interview months later that she thought a spirit of infirmity was linked to old and tired. As she received deliverance, many spirits seemed to leave like coveys of quail. She said that as we rebuked the main spirit, a whole group of spirits would go at the same time. A particular strong demon was Leviathan. This spirit caused her to twist, knocking her out of her chair onto the floor. But, because of the authority we have as believers to use the Name of Jesus, this spirit came out. Now, she says she is "energized" and is starting to do the work of a normal 30-year-old. As an interesting side note, a few weeks after Carrie's deliverance, her little three-year-old came over to her mother and said, "Mama, I feel real tired." Carrie immediately said to her daughter, "old and tired, are you there?" Her little daughter said, "Yes, I feel it in my tummy." Because Carrie had experienced deliverance, she used the Name of Jesus and commanded the "old and tired" spirit to come out using a very conversational tone, so that she did not frighten her three-year-old. The spirit immediately left and Carrie has not seen any more chronic tiredness with herself or her daughter. She is free to be and do what God has called her to do as an attorney and mother.

Death by Drugs

Carl, of Dallas, Texas, was born again when he attended high school but never grew much in the faith. He started experimenting with cocaine and became addicted. He reported in the interview for ministry that something seemed to be overpowering him. He thought this presence was going to kill him. Carl called a pastor friend of his in Oklahoma, that he had grown up with, Pastor Ted Mercer. The pastor suggested going to Deliverance Ministries because he had seen results for others. During Carl's ministry, the demons actually spoke out of his mouth. They announced their mission of death by drugs. A witchcraft spirit said that it came in when he played certain guitar music (a door to the spirit realm). At one point, that spirit moved Carl's hands to place them over his ears because we were quoting Luke 10:19, "we have power over all the enemy." The spirit did not want to hear it. As we used the Name of Jesus, we commanded the spirits to go to the feet of Jesus for judgment, and some of the spirits screamed loudly. Carl was set free in one session and is still free from drug addiction today. He reports that he has no desire for drugs. He has truly overcome by the authority in the Name of Jesus, the blood of the Lamb and the Word of His testimony.

A Generational Death Curse

Kristi strayed away from life in Christ for more than a decade after she was born again at the age of 10. She finally rededicated her life to Jesus about a year before I interviewed her. She had received some inner healing; however, she still had some tormenting problems with her and her children. After she rededicated her life to Jesus, she came to Deliverance Ministries and was shocked to experience various evil spirits manifesting by speaking out of her mouth. One spirit confessed that it was operating through a four-generation curse of death coming from and through the mother's family. Kristi pointed out how her oldest daughter had been plagued with infirmities since birth. She had major surgeries as a child. Kristi was tormented with a "night terror" spirit, causing her to see things in the house and be terrified. After forgiving various people, Kristi forgave herself. She experienced deliverance from several spirits of infirmity that had attacked her physical body for years. As a result, Kristi has seen other family members set free from oppression and healed.

Kristi's mother-in-law was healed from level three ovarian cancer through deliverance. The mother-in-law felt the cancer spirit leave her body physically during ministry. The doctors have confirmed that she is now cancer-free.

Frozen Neck Healed

Lisa, of Tulsa, Oklahoma, suggested that her son, Mark, come for ministry because of addiction to drugs and alcohol. Also, he wanted to see if the constant problems with his cars might be demonic. As it turns out, that is exactly what it was. Not only was he set free from the addictions, but a destroyer spirit disclosed it was there to destroy his vehicles. Jesus set him free that night at Deliverance Ministries. This led to a chain of supernatural events. Mark's wife watched and witnessed all this happen with positive results. His wife decided that she should come for ministry. She had a frozen neck, the result of a car accident 2-1/2 years before. Doctors were unable to help her medically or surgically. That night, the deliverance team laid hands on her according to scripture in Mark 16:17, speaking healing to her neck. Immediately, she started moving her head up and down and sideways with no pain! New x-rays later revealed the reality of her healing. A bone chip that had been floating in her neck, touching a nerve, now has been reattached supernaturally! Lisa stated in an interview with me several months later that this changed all their lives forever. In fact, Lisa decided to be trained, and became a team leader so that she could help others to receive the freedom and healing she was experiencing.

Smoking and Anger

Dr. Bill, a dentist, was born again at the age of six as his grandmother led him to Jesus. Jesus baptized him with the Holy Spirit, with the evidence of speaking in tongues, many years later. He reported in an interview with me that he physically felt the Holy Spirit come upon him in the form a wind blowing. However, he was plagued with smoking for 20 years. Because he wanted to be free from the addiction to nicotine, he came to a Deliverance Ministries session. He was ministered to by a couple who declared, by faith, that he would never smoke again … and Dr. Bill has not! There was a demon that showed up in his room one night later, announcing its name as "smoking." Dr. Bill knew he was free. As he simply rebuked the spirit, in the Name of Jesus, it turned around and left the room. Dr. Bill was delighted that he was also delivered from anger.

Marriage Under Attack

Phyllis had been a born again Christian for about five years at the time of the interview with Deliverance Ministries. She had grown in the Lord. Her husband lagged behind and would not attend Bible studies with his wife. All of a sudden, men began to pursue her and flirt with her at work regularly. For various reasons, she finally succumbed to the constant bombardment of temptation, having an affair with one man with whom she worked. Soon, she discovered he was in organized crime and dropped him like a rock. Then, she moved in with another man, and went to Las Vegas with him. In the meantime, her husband became desperate and came to Deliverance Ministries' office with a friend. In the prayer of agreement, Phyllis was lifted up in prayer and the spirits were bound. We believed and declared that she would return home. We asked angels to go and bring her home. We found out later that the very moment of our prayer of agreement, Phyllis started packing her bag to come home. The man she was with asked, "What are you doing?" She said, "I'm going home." He said, "Why?" Phyllis replied, "I don't know." Once she was home, Phyllis received deliverance, herself. During her deliverance, she reported that she thought she felt something moving in her brain when the evil spirits were leaving. Jesus set her free and her marriage is now better than ever!

A 13-Generation Witchcraft Spirit

Paige was born again at seven years of age. She was filled with the Holy Spirit at 18. However, because of intense spiritual warfare, she fell away from the Lord. She had no tools to overcome. She found herself tormented with drugs, anorexia, bulimia, depression, and witchcraft. When her husband divorced her, she knew she needed to get refocused on the reality of the Gospel and begin to hold on to Jesus. Much later, a friend told her about Deliverance Ministries. Paige thought she would go and get some help. At the conclusion of the teaching that evening, when the question was asked, "How many would like ministry tonight?" Paige put her hand up. Once into ministry, Paige was surprised that various spirits actually spoke out of her mouth. One evil spirit identified itself as a witchcraft spirit that had come through her mother's family and had been in the family for 13 generations! Paige now says that she was set completely free that evening. "I felt ten times lighter." She commented, "If only I had come many years before that eventful night." She told me many family relationships have now been restored. Her 10-year-old daughter was healed of arthritis that evening. This was most exciting. Paige is now ministering to others and seeing deliverance take place as people are set free from drugs, alcohol, smoking, and other spirits of darkness.

Healed of Lupus

Jackie was not sure about this type of ministry. She attended a traditional church that did not preach deliverance. However, she was ready to try anything because she was so sick. She felt she was going to die. Her stepdaughter and her husband kept insisting she must go to Deliverance Ministries. She had been diagnosed with Lupus and was getting worse every day. She was tormented with major pain in the joints, lower back pain, insomnia, fatigue, depression, fever, bad migraine headaches, and a sun rash. She could no longer ride in a car any distance at all. Jackie said her most dramatic moment in the Deliverance Ministries session was when the Bible was placed on her lower back and we asked the Holy Spirit to fill her. She said, "I felt a warmth in my lower back, like a hot heating pad, and spread upward throughout my body. My whole body was hot. That is when I knew I was completely healed. I felt so good." She saw immediate changes that day from the Lupus, pain, and other problems. She even slept great that night. Now, she is not concerned about dying.

Lesbian Set Free

Connie had been a born again Christian 11 years and filled with the Holy Spirit nine years before deliverance. However, she still had no victory over her lesbian activity. She had been a lesbian since she was 16. Her sister suggested she contact Deliverance Ministries. She progressed through the ministry of forgiving others and breaking ungodly soul ties, including all past sexual partners. She also experienced supernatural inner healing of various traumas in her past. Connie was surprised that certain evil spirits actually spoke through her mouth. In fact, the homosexual spirit announced itself as the head demon, having control over other evil spirits oppressing her life. She felt many spirits move up from her stomach physically. She felt some came out the top of her head. In total, around three dozen spirits were cast out. Connie said, "I have not felt this good since I was a child. No more plaguing sexual thoughts and nightmares. No struggle at all!" A year has passed since her ministry and Connie still remains free! Thank You, Jesus.

Homosexual Set Free

Ray was born again nine years before my interview with him after he had received deliverance ministry. He was tormented with homosexuality. Something just seemed to be controlling him. Ray said, "I was sick and tired of this lifestyle." Ray told me in the interview that he knew homosexuality was wrong. He knew what the scriptures said. When he listened to the radio show by Deliverance Ministries, he called and scheduled a ministry session.

The team that worked with Ray led him through repentance, renunciation of homosexuality, and rededication to Jesus. He said he could feel the spirits in a physical sensation as heaviness in his chest. As they came out, Ray stated that he felt "lighter and lighter." Jesus set him free! After his deliverance, Ray went through the deliverance ministry training and became a team leader to set others free of their problems.

Witchcraft, Drugs, Alcohol

Scott was delivered five years after being born again and filled with the Holy Spirit with the evidence of speaking in tongues. Scott previously played around with witchcraft, séances, and saw supernatural demonic activity. He was tormented by drug addiction, alcohol addiction, anger, rage, and perversity. Scott said he could feel these spirits in his physical body. He finally called out to Jesus for freedom. When Scott came to Deliverance Ministries, the spirits manifested and spoke out of his own mouth. He later told me, "These spirits took control of my mouth. They disclosed that some of the spirits were generational spirits and some were there because other people had spoken curses over me." Scott had several deliverance sessions. He felt more free each time he received ministry. In the end, he told me, "If I had not gone through deliverance, I don't believe I could have had the peace and power that I have now."

Voices of Suicide

A decade after Willie was in the armed service, he started feeling confused and alone. Strange thoughts continued to come into his head. He felt physical manifestations of knots moving up his arms. His stomach churned and then voices told him to destroy himself. Willie talked to several ministers; however, none of these ministers knew how to help him. Willie was not sure he was born again. Once, he heard voices encouraging him to drive up I-35 until he ran out of gas. The voices then prompted him to run up and down the highway. The voices said, "Take yourself out." Later, he responded to the voice telling him to cut his wrist. Willie wound up in the VA hospital psychiatric ward. When he was released from the psychiatric ward, he came to Deliverance Ministries. We led Willie to receive Jesus as His Lord and Savior and he was filled with the Holy Spirit and received deliverance. He felt better for a while. He started to read the Bible for the first time. But, shortly afterwards, he had a relapse, winding up again in the VA hospital psychiatric ward again. When I heard about this incident from his dad, I drove over to see him at the hospital. Willie was not aware I was coming, but a spirit was saying to him, "We do not want you around this guy." At the same time these voices were speaking to him, Willie had a terrible pain in his head. When I showed up, he understood what the voices were talking about. He finally learned how to do spiritual warfare ... casting down imaginations, taking every thought captive to the obedience of Jesus, testing the spirits that were speaking to him. Jesus set him free from the voices and he is free today. I want us to understand that Satan wins some suicide assignments. However, he lost this one. Sometimes it takes more than one ministry session before total freedom comes. In addition, each of us needs to learn how to test the spirits who are speaking to us to see if they are of God. And, we need to learn how to use the Name of Jesus to take every thought captive.

Back Healed

Buddy is a medical doctor, a podiatrist, and a businessman. He was born again in his mid-thirties and filled with the Spirit. He watched many deliverances, seeing manifestations of evil spirits. Buddy was a witness to people's lives being changed by the anointing of the Holy Spirit in this type of ministry. Nevertheless, because of his focus on medicine, when his back went out he didn't think of the supernatural. He thought he had pulled a muscle and chose to go to a chiropractor, but that didn't help. Several days passed by without relief. He was miserable. He had trouble breathing. He had trouble getting out of bed. Buddy and I started to talk about his problem. I suggested that I come over to pray ... Buddy agreed. After dealing with some unforgiveness, I checked his limbs. I discovered that one leg was short. I commanded the spine to adjust in Jesus' Name and commanded the pain to go. His legs began to move and ended up being the same length as the result of his spine lining up with the Word of God. When, Buddy stood up, the pain was gone! He said he was shocked. He admitted that previously, the only thing he thought of was medical treatment for his healing. He didn't think about the healing power of the Holy Spirit released in Jesus' Name.

Anorexia

Lauren, a born again Christian teenager living in the Ft. Worth area, had been diagnosed with anorexia, an eating disorder. She lost 40 pounds as a petite young woman. The doctors told the family that this problem would be with her the rest of her life. However, she and her parents were convinced it was demonic because Lauren was hearing voices. She allowed these voices to control her because she didn't know how to fight them. She told me in our interview that when she attempted to eat something, the voices would tell her she that was unworthy. Consequently, she would feel guilty and not eat. The voices told her that she would be punished if she ate. Furthermore, when the family scheduled her to go to Deliverance Ministries in Oklahoma City, the spirits told her that they would kill her if she went. Concerned as she was, Lauren felt she could not continue with the status quo. On the way to Oklahoma City, she told her parents to be ready to call 911 once they arrived for ministry. Going through the preparation for ministry, unforgiveness was discovered. She had broken up with an old boyfriend. She forgave him and herself, then broke the ungodly soul tie with him. All of the ministry itself was very routine. In fact, the spirits were as quiet as a mouse. When we finished, Lauren seemed to be more outgoing and expressed that she was hungry! We were all excited to hear her say this! They stopped at a cafeteria before leaving Oklahoma City for Ft. Worth. She ate well. At home, her dad made up her favorite dish of spaghetti and meatballs. However, about a week later there were some demonic manifestations at the home where the spirits talked out of her mouth. Lauren admitted she had opened some doors to the spirit world, allowing spirits to come back in. During these manifestations Lauren and her parents rose to the occasion because they had learned who they are in Jesus and the power they have in His Name. They immediately cast out the spirits and that was the end of it! Lauren has been free since, eating freely now. The doctors gave her a clean bill of health. She says her whole life has turned around!

Who do you know who has some of the same problems shown in these testimonies? The power in Jesus is ready when the person is ready.

CHAPTER 19

EXORCISING HOMES, BUILDINGS OR LAND

From time to time, Deliverance Ministries is asked to expel "ghosts" or demons from a home, building, or land. The person calling us usually starts the conversation on the telephone by saying something like, "You are not going to believe this." I always say, "Oh, yes I will."

Most of the time, people do not have anyone to talk to about spiritual problems like this. They are afraid that other people will think that they are crazy. Sometimes pastors are not helpful, thinking and saying, "Christians cannot be bothered by demons." I always tell people that they can talk freely at Deliverance Ministries.

A young couple called me from Yukon, Oklahoma, just west of Oklahoma City. They had something in the house like a "ghost" bothering them and their children. In the kitchen they watched water faucets turn on by themselves. Cabinet doors opened and slammed shut. This was brought to a head was when evil spirits started shaking the children's beds in the night, waking them up and scaring them. The parents finally called Deliverance Ministries. They shared with me that one night the wife had awakened to see a dark form at the end of the bed speaking with a deep voice saying, "Serve Satan." I told her, "At least it was clean cut. You know who was speaking to you." It is not always so obvious. Some demons will pose as an angel of light; that is, they will act like one of God's angels, attempting to throw the listener off track.

Instead of going to their home, I suggested they go through our Monday evening teaching and ministry session first. When they came in, I was able to work with them. They went through the door-closing prayer and dealt with unforgiveness. I joined with them in agreement concerning their house and property, dedicating the house to the Lord Jesus and renouncing and rebuking any demonic activity with them or their home. We declared Luke

10:19, stating that we have ALL power in Jesus' name and that nothing would harm us. We asked God's angels to be of service to us (Hebrews 1:14) and sweep through the house, pulling out any demonic entities and dropping them at the feet of Jesus for judgment.

This report came back later: The torment was gone and the husband was delivered from chewing tobacco. This was a case where we did not even go to the property ... power in the Name of Jesus worked even at a distance as we have read about in the Bible! It seems that our ministry has become known as the local "ghost busters." Because we are willing, God does seem to use us as a "special ops" or "commando unit."

Some years ago, a CPA friend of mine called about some strange things going on in their house. Doors had been slamming shut and clothes were coming off the rack by themselves. One night while they were asleep, a water pipe broke upstairs and filled the house with water ... they had to move out while the insurance company paid for the total remodel. Once the remodel was completed and they were ready to move back in, they called for ministry, as they did not want it to happen again.

While I was on the phone talking to the wife, she heard the upstairs toilet flush all by itself. She was alone her quiet home. We laughed, figuring that the evil spirits knew what was going on and had decided to go ahead and flush themselves down the toilet!

When my wife and I met with the husband and wife at their home, I asked them if they had anything in the house that might give the demons (ghosts) any rights to torment them in their home. They said, "No, but when we moved in there was a pentagram painted on the upstairs bedroom ... we painted over it!"

That was the clue we were looking for. I had the husband as the spiritual head, with his wife in agreement, dedicate the home to the Lord Jesus Christ. I asked them to renounce all demonic activity, to neutralize the pentagram and all witchcraft that took place in the home previously. I asked them to command all demons to go to the feet of Jesus and report for judgment. We asked the angels of God Almighty to check throughout the house and cleanse it spiritually.

They had no more demonic activity.

I received a call from an employee at a hospital on the south side of Oklahoma City. The administration office had a "ghost" bothering the employees, especially at night. Some employees were refusing to work the night shift. They thought it might be a "female ghost," because it seemed to have a perfume smell with it. When the "ghost" was active, there was a coldness present and a few employees actually bumped into the entity. One male employee was hit on the head when something came off a shelf all by itself. Another strange thing was happening: something was turning on a computer that listed the hospital patients … and was working with it as people watched! Weird!?!

So they called the "ghost busters" organization in town, Deliverance Ministries, for help. I suggested to the employee that I would mail some prayer cloths to them. We have used prayer cloths quite a bit through the years with great success. In Acts 19:12, Paul used handkerchiefs to minister to many, which resulted in healing and deliverance. As born again Christians, we can do the same as we pray and anoint the prayer cloth in the name of Jesus. These prayer cloths are like spiritual hand grenades to the enemy.

I told the assistant manager on the telephone to try these first. If needed, we would bring one of our SWAT teams (Spiritual Warfare Attack Team) and address the "ghost"; i.e., spirit of darkness.

About ten days later, I got a letter that the "ghost" activity had disappeared.

CHECKLIST FOR EXORCISING A HOME, BUILDINGS OR LAND

- It is always good to suggest the owner(s) go through deliverance for a broader sweep on the problem, in any case, breaking any curses including on the land.
- Have the owner(s) dedicate the home or place to the Lord Jesus, the Christ, declaring the blessings of the new covenant and declaring that this is holy ground.
- Repent of any sin that has taken place there, asking for forgiveness.
- Ask the Lord to show you any ouija boards, or other witchcraft objects, books, satanic games, etc., that are giving rights for demons.
- Renounce and rebuke any witchcraft or other demonic activity of the past or present (Rituals, suicides, severe traumas, crimes).
- Sometimes a so-called "ghost" that people see is actually a demon that is posing as a person who has died. (This is called a "familiar spirit") These demons know a lot about the deceased. In any case, renounce it and rebuke it.
- Ask God's angels to sweep through the place, pulling out the demonic activity.
- Lastly, I often go around the home, building, or land, anointing it with blessed oil in the Name of the Father, Jesus, the Christ, and the Holy Spirit. Also, I go around rebuking any remaining demonic activity, **declaring that Jesus is Lord here!**

CHAPTER 20

MULTIPLE PERSONALITIES

TRUE MULTIPLE PERSONALITIES ARE NOT DEMONS

In the earlier years of my ministry I used to think that multiple personalities had to be demons. Somewhere along the way, I understood this problem and how it works. I came to the realization that multiple personalities, alter-personalities, disassociate identity disorders (DID) or protectors are actually a God-send for the child who is experiencing traumas their psyche is not able to handle. These traumas, in most every case, have to do with sexual abuse.

As children grow up, they experience traumas that they cannot handle. During the experience, their intellect and creativity kick in, creating an alternate personality (I'm going to call them protectors). These protectors protect them from the bad memories. Sometimes, they have a different name. In extreme cases, the person does not even know what is going on. They don't know what they are doing when they are acting out of a different personality. Sometimes, there is a time lapse when the individual has lost several hours during the period of time that the protector was in control. Other times, the individual is hearing a voice or voices from the protectors as they try to protect them. As a result, they experience a lot of confusion. And, of course, demons can be mixed into the middle of all this activity. Sometimes demons are speaking; other times, the protector is speaking. Our Jesus wants us to be ONE, integrated completely with one mind and to have our mind renewed with the Word of God (2 Corinthians 13:11 and Romans 12:2). He wants us to be an integrated whole.

You may want to attempt to establish communication with a protector when you are ministering to people who tell you about sexual abuse they are aware of, or if you are suspicious that they have experienced sexual abuse. (In the less extreme situations, it may be that an inner child is speaking through the individual. They may be and acting out of that inner child. You can treat the protector and the inner child the same way. When speaking to the protector or the inner child **ask Jesus to cleanse and heal them** of emotional wounds, including cleansing and healing of the protectors.)

It is most important to be aware that there may be false protectors; i.e., demons posing as protectors. I always declare, "If there are any false protectors acting out the protector role, confess before the Lord Jesus that you are a demon and not a protector." Based on the answer that I get, I ask, "Do you confess this to be true before the Lord Jesus Christ?" If there are demons posing as protectors, then I ask God's angels to come and deal with them, asking them to drop these demons at the feet of Jesus for judgment.

I usually start out by saying, "Is there an inner child or protector present that I can visit with?" If there is no response I will say, "It's okay to visit with me, I'm a friend of _____ and I am here to help. I belong to Jesus, so I am ministering to _____. I know you are not a demon and that you are here to protect _____. I want you to know how much we appreciate all that you have done for _____. You have been helping her (it's usually a female) to cope with all that she has been through. Will you visit with me?" If I still do not get a response but I am pretty sure they are there, I **ask Jesus to talk to the protectors** about visiting with me. Then I just wait.

If communication is finally established with the protector (often there will be a child's voice responding), I normally ask, "How old are you?" If you can get an age, I then ask, "Do you have a name?" You may or may not get a name; many times all you get is an age. Then I ask, "How many protectors are present?" In a typical case, there would be about six to twelve. I say, "Can I visit with the oldest or someone who can speak for the group?" If you don't get another one up, then continue with this one. "Can the other protectors hear me?" They usually can hear me. "How many of you know Jesus?" This is a good time to **ask Jesus to come talk to them** about who He is and for all of the protectors to receive Him into their hearts, since they are part of the person. If they are not ready to receive Jesus, then **ask Jesus to talk to them** some more about who He is and to share the Gospel.

When the protectors have all agreed to make Jesus their Lord, then lead them through a simple child-like prayer, asking Jesus to come into their hearts, give their life to Him and forgive them of any sins. Then, I tell the protectors that I will come back to them later after the dark ones, or demons, are gone.

Now I like to move into the deliverance process. I am assuming the person seeking deliverance has gone through the door-closing prayer, soul tie prayers and inner healing. If you are able to get the head demon up, sometimes it will disclose how many true protectors are there. The head demon will also disclose if any demons are still there, posing as true protectors. If you discover there are some false protectors, rebuke the demons posing as protectors and send them to the feet of Jesus. If you are unable to get the head demon up, work the suspect list and just do normal deliverance.

After deliverance, call the protector (the one speaking for the group) back up. I like to ask them if they can tell that the dark ones or demons are now gone. The protectors can usually tell if they are gone. If they are aware that demons are still there, do more deliverance as needed.

This would be a good time to recheck for any additional inner healing of emotional wounds, asking Jesus to show them an event or memory that yet needs healing. Some of the protectors may be blocking the memories. Ask Jesus to talk to the protectors about unblocking these memories, if needed. If the person then locks onto something, go ahead and do inner healing.

Now, **ask Jesus to visit with the protectors about walking** into the white light of the Holy Spirit within the person. (The protectors seem to always see the light or an entry.) It is possible that Jesus may not want to integrate all of them at once. In my experience, this is rare. I have had protectors say, "I do not want to die." If they say this, **ask Jesus to speak His truth to them about this.** (They are not going to die, of course, but simply make the person whole.)

When the protectors say they are ready, then I just thank them and tell them to go ahead and walk into the white light of the Holy Spirit. *Always say goodbye to them.*

PROTECTOR/ALTER/MPD/DID/SRA CHECKLIST

1. ESTABLISH COMMUNICATION WITH HEAD DEMON – IDENTIFY AND CONFIRM, INTIMIDATE WITH GOD'S ANGELS. (If unable to get head demon up with good communication, do steps 3-8.)

2. Interrogate the head demon. Find out how many protectors are present and how many false protectors are present, if any. Take authority over the false protectors (who are actually demons) and cast them out sending them to the feet of Jesus. Use God's angels as necessary while casting them out. Confirm with the head demon that the false protectors are gone. Interrogate the head demon to find out the most senior protector (usually the oldest).

3. Put the head demon on standby and call up the most senior protector. If you can establish a clear line of communication with the protector, thank it for its help coping with the traumas ... "we really appreciate you for all that has been done to help through the years." Tell it that we know it is not a demon and that we will visit with it later. (Sometimes the spokesman protector; i.e., the most senior protector, can help in the deliverance by calling it back up and asking it what it sees in the spiritual world.) If a clear line of communication was not established with the most senior protector, then go to the next protector until a good flow of communication is going. A spokesman needs to be established so that you can work with it as a leader over the other protectors (there could be thousands of protectors). Finally, put it on standby. Ask Jesus to commence the cleansing process by visiting with the protectors about who He is. Ask Jesus to share the Gospel message and visit with them about opening up the traumatic memories to receive inner healing later. At this point, call the head demon back up and proceed with deliverance as outlined in the "Head demon technique" OR do basic deliverance.

4. After the deliverance is completed, call the spokesman protector back up. Confirm that the other protectors can hear the conversation you are having with the protector spokesman. If they can't hear you, have the senior protector relay information to them. Ask them if they would like to ask Jesus into their hearts so they can be born again. Tell them the person they are protecting has already received Jesus as Lord and Savior. When they are ready, lead them in a simple salvation prayer. Ask them if their clothes have become white. If their clothes are not white, ask questions to determine what is going on. Have all of them received Jesus as their Lord and Savior? Is there a false protector

(demon) present that has been overlooked? Cast it out. Is a demon or demons attached to a particular protector, such as doubt, unbelief, deception or anti-christ. Cast these out.

5. Discuss the idea of them integrating into the host so they can all serve Jesus together as one. If they are unsure about this (sometimes they will say, "We don't want to die"), ask Jesus to talk to them about it. Give Jesus time to speak to them. That will usually do it. Tell the senior protector to report that they are ready to become one. Ask if they can see the white light of the Holy Spirit within the person. If they can't see it (which is rare), ask Jesus to make it clear.

6. Ask them to hold hands together. If there are baby protector(s), pick them up so they can be carried. If there are hundreds or thousands of protectors, they may need to be fused into the spokesman protector so that the process is orderly. Coordinate all of this with the spokesman protector.

7. Finally, thank them and say goodbye as they walk into the white light of the Holy Spirit.

8. At the end, do inner healing as the Holy Spirit leads.

CPSIA information can be obtained
at www.ICGtesting.com
Printed in the USA
BVHW020157230623
666255BV00009B/541